The STORY
of the PEOPLE

EILEEN M. ROTA

THE STORY OF THE PEOPLE

by
Eileen M. Rota

The
STORY
of the
PEOPLE

Published by
Light Technology
P.O. Box 1526
Sedona, Arizona   86339

Library of Congress
Catalog Card Number: 93-080766
ISBN 0-929385-51-9

Cover Art by Janneke Verster

Printed by
Mission Possible Commercial Printing
P.O. Box 1495
Sedona, Arizona   86339

Dedicated to Ilyaphlebian.

My deepest gratitude is extended to Julia Fierman and Steve Whitman for their Light-filled presence during the forty-one channeled sessions, and to Phyllis Whitney, Skip and Fay Atwater, and Don Delaney for their generous support and encouragement during the writing and following self-transformative time. Thank you to O'Ryin Swanson, publisher and friend, for trusting the goosebumps and hair-standing-on-end while we talked, and for being the "maker of the words on paper." Surely together we all have carried this story into your hands.

Contents

Part Three: The Story of the People

Illustrations by Janneke Verster

Preface

The walkway through the ancient Indian burial mounds pulled me past in quiet respect, through to the circle of tree stumps where I sat for a while. I had made my peace with the spirits who dwelled here the last time I had been atop this mountain in Woodstock, New York, and now felt comfort in sensing their presence. It was riding on that serenity that the message came loudly and clearly: "Go to the meditation room. Go now."

Where many teachings had been spoken, tears shed, laughter and love shared during the recent retreat, the meditation room was now empty except for me. As my meditations were usually deep and quiet, perhaps it was because of the habit of preparing for group sessions that I turned on the recording equipment and pinned the mic to my sweater. It wasn't until two hours later that I was grateful for that robot-like action.

After some deep breaths, I sat quietly and the visions began. Eight golden lines flowed outward, reconverged, and burst their ending at a black dot, like a location on a map. The black dot opened like a flower and in it, pointing upward, was a spear. Flowing from the top of the spear were red pieces of material flying in the wind.

Then one came to speak to me as two buffalo flew above us. His brown face was so close to me that his great headdress filled his entire aura. His name came to me as Mekh-Tuckh, Flying Bull, and then the knowingness that bull meant buffalo.

The words were spoken to me: "Your journey."

The vision continues. The wind is blowing tattered blue cloth which catches upon some black weeds or stalks, black as if they had been burned. Under the weeds is a piece of gold. It is a neck-piece and in the center is a gold carving of wings going straight upward. Now it becomes an eagle. It's an eagle, a Golden Eagle.

I ask in my mind, "What is this message, what is the guidance? You called me to sit here. Now I am here. What do you say?" The vision continues.

I still see the headdress with brown and white fur. There are many, many

Indians coming around, all doing something different. One has on him some sticks and upon the sticks are feathers and furs, trailing long behind him. He is dancing as if they are wings. He has a great bird head on his own head and he is dancing around.

I wonder where my White Chief is. I've called him that ever since he appeared in the East corner of my own meditation room on the day I was smudging and chanting. There he stood with his huge white headdress and all white skins. When we met, I knew I'd known him forever. As I remember that time long ago, he appears in my vision. Coming down the mountain, he takes my hand and pulls me up, saying, "Come." We travel up the mountain very fast, barely touching the ground, until an opening in the mountain appears. Here were enter and travel through a tunnel. We're going so fast that the wind is rushing past my ears. I don't recall ever before traveling this fast with him. He still holds my hand as we go through the tunnel.

The tunnel weaves around, turns and bends to the right, and we still continue. It's as if we're going in and in and then down and down like streaks of light into the blue darkness. It's a long journey. I ask, "Where are we going?" He grips my hand tighter and we go on. I have a feeling that we are going to the Land Within the Earth, and as the thought finishes, we are standing at an opening and there it is, the Land Within. It's so very beautiful, very large, as if it were a great, huge cavern.

There's a kind of urgency in my hurried walking on a path, as I push aside the branches of the trees. The momentum carries me to the clearing. I can see them in my mind before I even arrive. The Great Ones are standing in full light, standing.

One is as if a great bird, yet a man. One is as if a great cat, yet a man. There is one who is a wolf, yet a man. It is the bird before me and to the left is a man with a bear on him. Then stands the wolf man, there's another to my left, yet out of view. To the right of the bird is one who is a cat, a mountain cat, and beside him there is another, a big black cat. Next to him is a standing lizard man.

There seems to be something like a carpet stretching across the circle between me and the bird man. As I move to the center, my wonderful White Warrior stands behind me. I begin to spin around. We all spin, accelerating in speed and taking the form of a wheel. I am at the hub and I see spokes curving outward to the rim. The place beneath my feet opens and I begin lowering, lowering into the Earth through that very center spot. They swirl around and enter behind me.

I am standing, with my arms by my sides, in a darkness. The pull to make some toning sounds enters and next that is exactly what I do, sounds rising higher and higher in pitch and then going back down, like a pulsebeat. Then I feel his presence. His face is wide and brown as if he is comprised of the Earth itself. He speaks.

"This place be the center of the center of the Earth. From within this depth we speak. There are those who have traveled upon the surface of the Earth and believed that their love and knowingness of the surface have given them the knowingness of the Earth; and we say, 'Until you have traversed to the center within the Earth, you have little comprehension of what is Earth and what is the vibration of Earth.' Here in the core, in the depth of the Earth, reside the Ones who first did place their feet within the Earth.

"Those who first did place their feet, did so within, in deep caverns. Here they did reside. Upon the twelfth year of their residing were they then carried through the tunnel, toward the surface, that they might experience the skin of the Earth. There were those who journeyed upon the skin and who chose to remain. There were those who breathed the air within the skin and did choose to return to the center.

"Within the core is carried the knowingness that the Earth will spin upon itself, thus shaking itself free beyond that which is called the skin. Nothing will remain upon the surface. It has occurred again and again. Now, through the breathings of the universe, it begins again. There are whose who will enter within. There are those who will lift themselves through beams of light to other locations whilst the Earth does burn and cleanse itself free, to begin anew. Fool not yourselves that you will remain on the surface. None will remain on the surface.

"Those who choose to enter and journey within will then begin to feel the movement of the Earth. There are those who will present themselves and call you to enter. No thinking will decide for you. Your heart will move your feet, as of old. Then will you enter, for there are those who enter who did begin at the first changing, long ago, to enter within during the Great Turning."

For a moment he speaks directly to me: "Your Story of the People will speak the words. They will hear. Those beings will hear. They will find the words and read and hear. The People of the Earth beg to hear the story, beg to read the story, beg to see the story. Their hearts ache to hear the story."

The strength of his words fill my senses as he continues, "Then on this speaking do we call upon those ones to gather the Story of the People within their arms and feel their hearts moved, that it might be written on paper for all to read, that it might be made into living visions that all might see again and again, that their hearts might be stirred. This be the greatest epic ever told.

"Oh peoples of Earth, hear your story, receive your story, breathe your story. It has been spoken. The Story of the People. You have written it well. Now, upon the wings of the bird does it fly to the hands of one who will carry it to the people on paper and on moving visions, both...both. The bear does dance, standing with its great being. The great mountain cat does dance. Cat of blackness does dance. Lizard's tongue does dance. The goat does dance. The wolf does dance. The great spinning does spin. The breathing, the breath of the fires, essence, does blow forth from the center of the Earth. Let the Story be known."

He looks upward through the tunnel, toward the surface. "Then we call them: 'Know you who you are. Receive those words from the depths and the core of the Earth, do we speak to you. The circle spins. The calling begins. Be you who you are. Be you who you are. Gather yourselves together, we call you: makers of moving visions, words upon paper call we. Let the Light be known, let the Light be known, let the Light be known. Oh Ones be true, alter not the Story."

"You who stand atop the vortex, hear these words." I look up and see many chiefs of many peoples encircling the top, standing with the outstretched arms and open hands held together facing upward, as if to receive. He continues, "The Story comes, many hearts will be filled, many hearts will be filled.

"Then the call has been spoken. Let it be so upon the skin of the Earth. Let it be so."

I didn't remember leaving the core of the Earth or the journey toward consciousness. I simply awakened. Time resumed its own keeping. The visions were complete, the message was complete. "Thank you," I repeated softly again and again as I rocked my body.

Upstairs, I found Bella stirring soup in the kitchen. She had worked with the Indians who had created the sweat lodge and the peace walk amongst the ancient burial mounds. I smiled as I walked toward her, knowing she was the right person at the right time. "I have to speak aloud my vision. Will you hear it?"

"I thought I saw you go down to the meditation room alone. Yes, tell me."

There we stood, together in the kitchen, while I repeated back to her the vision, remembering especially the calling of the peoples to come forth and receive the story. When I had finished, we both stood quietly.

She again slowly stirred the soup and looked back to me, "Have you ever heard the story of the White Buffalo?"

"No, I haven't." I felt my consciousness change a little as she began.

"The Indian history tells of the White Buffalo who speaks through a white woman, and it is a white woman who brings the real history, the real story, back to the Indians. Are you sure you've never heard it before?" She looked from her soup to me.

I heard my mouth say, "That's me. That's who I am." My hand covered my mouth. "I had no idea I would say that!" She smiled.

Before I left Bella's spiritual center to continue on my next journey, she gave me a card with a picture of the White Buffalo on the front, and inside she wrote, "Thank you for your divine presence." Blessed be Bella always.

Months later, I found myself driving west, across the deserts. My friend was sleeping beside me, and I glanced at her while I thought about the recent events that had led us to journey to Sedona, Arizona. I'd traveled where spirit guided for years, but I'd never been "out west." Now, here I was driving through the desert. An odd sensation gathered about me. It was as if two giant spirit wheels

formed on either side of the road. I could hear their thunder, their whirling...and then the whispering. "She is carrying the story to the people, she is
carrying the story to the people." Time stood still. I don't know how long the
whirling and whispering lasted, I don't know how far I drove, or if I was even
driving at all. I only knew that somehow I was doing just that, carrying the Story
to the People.

November, 1993
Eileen Rota

Emergence I

"They came. In the long tunnel leading into the abyss, there appeared a glimmer of light. First in one cavern and then in another, outlines of great stone tables came into view. And on the tables, sparkling particles of light appeared and multiplied. In each cavern, on each table, creation took form."

INTRODUCTION

The Calling

In the time marked on the planet called Earth once every millennium he comes and the calling begins. Now is that time; today is that day. Of those who have responded to the call, few have ever returned. And yet when his beckoning resounds throughout the universe, they come. "Hereupon we call the opening to begin," he thundered. "Turn aside! Let the doors be opened!"

The planet Earth knew well the familiar sound and with the ease of a breath she responded. She moved and stretched and yawned a little. And just where the base of the mountain began to rise, the mouth of the cave opened wide. There at this entryway he stood. Into the depths of the deepest caves he called forth. Into the caverns he breathed his breath of beckoning. Into the bowels of the great Earth he called to them. Softly at first, he whispered, "Gather together the essence of your being. Gather together the essence of your being." As if they were his children he coaxed them, "Come, here there is heart. Come, here there are ears. We have been waiting." As if they were his lovers he wooed them. "Yes, dear ones, yes, it is true. The time is here at last. For you have lain those bodies down. In slumber you have been, merely a shell. And now we call upon you to come to the Earth Mother once again. Come forth! Breath the breath of life."

The universe stirred. Again his great form reached outward toward the entryway. "Awaken in the depths! Awaken in the depths!" He called upon the others, "Oh Great Ones, oh Holy Ones, bring them forth! Bring them forth!"

They came. In the long tunnel leading into the abyss there appeared a glimmer of light. First in one cavern and then in another, outlines of great stone tables came into view. And on the tables sparkling particles of light appeared and multiplied. In each cavern on each table, creation took form. The glowing light of their bodies filled the caverns and spilled forth even to the entryway. He knew before he saw the light. He felt them at last. "Yes, dear ones, feel the life force flowing within you. Breathe the breath of life. Breathe the holy breath. Yes!"

The Earth cradled them in her womb. Once again they came to tell the truths, the grandness, the simplicity. And once again they came to speak their story: The Story of the People.

"Rest, dear ones, rest. Then we will beckon you to come forth." He soothed them, he blessed them, he loved them. "Oh Holy Ones," he called again, "stand at the gates and let none other enter. For these ones assimilate their beings, gathering the essence together, and take form in creation. Oh Great Ones, guard the gates."

As they rested his faint murmur passed over them, for there has been silence, and now the truth will be spoken once again...the journey forth begins.

With barely a movement they breathed while their bodies acclimated to the Earth. They had heard him call to the Holy Ones. They had felt the sealing of the gates. And now their spirits settled into the density of physical form. They rested for three days and three nights. On the morning of the fourth day they stirred. They felt the vibration of his commanding words. "Awaken, beloved ones. We beckon you from your slumber. Awaken! Awaken!" They stirred a little more and began to move their limbs.

As if a great father calling his children he spoke to them: "Dear ones, you know the time is at hand. Come forth. Come forth from the womb. None other has viewed the beauty of your beings. None other has felt your breath upon them. None other has felt your presence. Come, place your feet upon the Earth Mother."

And in the caverns deep within and beneath the mountain they began to rise. They stood like beacons, golden beings with their light ever increasing, glowing, filling the depths and flooding toward the entryway. He knew they were ready. The time had come. It was now.

"Come forth into the essence of life! Come forth, let the Mother feel you upon her again, for there has been silence and now the word will be spoken. Let the Story live again!" He rejoiced in the words.

They came walking from the wombs and through the passageways. One after another, meeting and forming a line, golden beings newly born moved toward the entryway where he awaited them. And even as he saw the first emerge from the depths into the light of day he wept. "Oh beloved People...oh beloved People, you have returned!"

His great arm motioned them forward as the numbers stepped outward until as many as fifty gathered before the wide expanse of field below. With just one stride he stood before them, so great was he. "See you the fields, golden as you?" He pointed to the edges of the field. "See you the trees, erect as you?" Bending low he whispered, "See you the expanse of sky upon which you have ridden? Feel you the Mother beneath your feet, around your being?"

Riding upon his words they stepped down the little rise and into the field. The grasses brushed against their legs the wind breathed a breath and kissed their cheeks. The Earth Mother felt them upon her once again. The People had returned.

None noticed as he quietly returned to the entryway and gave thanks to the Holy Ones. He crossed his raised arms. "The gates are closed!" And then so low and softly that none other heard, "Then let the caverns return to dust. Rest, great dwellings, rest. Rest, the depths. Rest, the depths. For you have held these great beings and now the story begins."

In union the People gathered together, encircling the great field. And when the circle was made complete, for a moment they paused and looked across and around at each other. Then without a signal or sign they began to walk the patterns of their truths.

No words were spoken. Not one veered one way or another but kept walking round and round the great circle and then across one way and then another. Until there formed a cross within the circle. Within the four segments of the circle different colors appeared. It was as if the colors flowed from their beings as they walked together. The first was entirely filled with blue, the color of the sea. And then within the blue formed a deep red circle. In the second was drawn what appeared to be the head of an arrow with one line extending and trailing behind. In the third a large glistening black ball and in the fourth one atop the other came three waving blue lines the color of the summer sky. And still they continued weaving patterns...throughout the daylight and even into the time of dusk. The light from their patterns shone forth and the entire universe saw golden patterns of light forming once again upon the Earth. Tirelessly they continued, forming one pattern and then another. First the cross and then as if a bud opening wide into a blossom and closing once again, they walked the living symbols of their truths.

And before him they formed a great wheel even unto the spokes and the hub. As they moved so did the wheel and the spokes curved like the spinning force they were and veered inward directly into the center of the hub. Each one followed the other walking around and then into the hub and back out to the circle. A living wheel they formed. And then a gift they presented before him: It was as if together they had actually become a great golden wheel. It began to lift and rise steadily and surely until at last it was raised upward and standing on its rim! Still it turned and moved, so alive was it, breathing and pulsating. He watched. The universe watched. Within the great wheel the People continued walking. Carried by the force, they flowed along the curved lines and as each entered the spinning vortex within the hub their golden bodies disappeared and became the sparkling essence from which they had come. They returned to essence! And then with the ease of breathing their bodies took form once again as they walked back out from the hub. This, then, was the living truth of the wheel: In union flowing to the center, returning to essence and then stepping back into form. When the very last in turn had walked to the center and returned, the wheel slowly and gently, with the grace of a leaf in the wind, lowered itself down. He watched as it reverted back to the circle of his beloved beings. Their gift was great.

Sacred Dance

"Then a great gift they presented him: It was as if together they had become a great wheel. Within the great wheel, the People continued walking."

The first words were spoken. She stepped forward, her eyes glistening, her smooth head and body glowing with golden light, carrying the radiance of new life upon her. She spoke to him and to the watching universe. "We are the People." Her voice was clear and strong. We have resounded with the beckoning and gathered our beings again. We have been waiting and heard the call and now stand before you. We now take form, the People. We have heard the words, 'Here there are ears, here there is heart.' Then we come once again in the forming of the new world. The telling of our story is the forming of a new world, for in the speaking is the creating. This Great Mother carries us all. There are many more in the caverns. Do you think that here there is only you and we? There are many still in slumber. They wait also." A ball of light formed between her hands. As she turned it from side to side, she repeated three times, "For the time comes when the great Earth Mother will shake herself free and begin anew." The light-ball disappeared as she opened her arms toward the Earth upon which she stood. "Oh Great Mother, we walk upon you once again! We place our feet upon you! We breathe the breath of life! We walk the patterns of truth in the light of day! From your bowels we have come. We honor you, oh Great Mother! We honor you! Blessed are we who place our feet upon you." Three times they chanted the words together. "Oh Great Mother! Oh Great Mother! Oh Great Mother!" And their mother felt them upon her, heard their words and returned their love. And then the one who had called came down into the field and walked amongst them. Even through their glowing light, the white brilliance from his right hand shone greater than all of them together. He held it up to be seen, and a nearly blinding light it was. His power and strength drew them to him. "Oh People, here you are once again." The resonance of his voice pulled them closer still. "Feel yourselves. Feel who you are." They were spellbound by the intensity of his presence. All the histories of the universe spoke of him, yet only after the beckoning could they actually experience his splendor. It was greater than the histories could foretell.

He sat upon the grassy knoll and spoke. "Here is everything. Do not call upon the others. Do not call upon those things you barely remember." With his words the histories and the memories of those they had known slipped away. His words electrified them. "Begin again. Begin anew!" He beseeched them, "Create nothing that is not of this Earth. Everything is here. Here you be, Great Ones. Grandness of heart. Innocence of being." They basked in his radiant love. "Here you be!"

And so the story begins. The People are taking form and coming forth from the bowels of the Earth carrying their innocence and strong hearts. As the darkness of night comes upon them, each one faces outward along the rim of the circle and crouches down a little. They begin moving their hands in small circles. White silken threads spill forth. It is as if they spin it from the space between their hands and their body. Back and forth they weave and soon each has before him a shimmering white cocoon.

Then, as quiet as a breath, they enter. Oval portals close behind as they lay their sleek bodies down. As children curling their bodies in upon themselves, they rest upon their Mother, feeling and moving with her breathing bosom. For the People do love the Mother beyond the words that are spoken here. And in the places where they had walked, the pulsating, changing patterns continue to radiate for the universe to see: Both in light and in dark the truths reside.

This is called the new beginning. And each knows, for only would they be beckoned forth at the new beginning.

Emergence II

"The holding place where they would live for the next thirty days called to them. Some walked around the field filled with flowers, others to the tall green trees, and a few to the riverbank."

Part One

The Gathering

CHAPTER ONE

The Purpose

At the first sign of dawn they pushed aside the cocoons and stood together. He watched as the full light broke upon them and they began the salutation. It was simple and without sound. He knew it well. In a circle, they firstly reached their smooth arms outward and paused. Then together they moved, placing their open hands in four positions: over the navel, over the heart, upon the shoulders, their arms crossing the chest, and above the head. In between each position they reached outward and paused. Three times their arms gracefully flowed through the patterns.

His heart filled with the sight. Everything was occurring as it should, as it had millennium after millennium. And yet...perhaps this time would be different. Perhaps. Now it was all up to them, his dear ones, the People. His work was finished. He watched as the Great One from amongst them stepped forward and revealed himself.

Like them his smooth head and body radiated golden light, yet when he spoke they knew he was the Great One who had journeyed with them. His gentle love nourished them. "Let this great golden field be our gathering place, lest we forget how we formed here. For those who have come before us have forgotten." He pointed in all directions. "Beyond this golden field, beyond these erect trees and blue sky there are those who have gone before us and have forgotten who they are!" A slight murmur lingered amongst them. "Yes, it is true," he continued. "There have been others who responded to the call. There were those who came even before the ones before us carrying the very same purposes." His heart remembered them all. "There are many. They too are the People!"

He read their thoughts and responded, "You think that you could not forget who you are. Yet those others thought the very same, and they did turn from themselves!"

His words were strong and powerful. "Then this is our first purpose: To maintain the truths. Here at each full Moon Mother we will gather together, one and all, to the very last, and walk the truths of light. In this way we will remember who we are and the truths will be maintained through the emanating light." He paused a moment and then added, "For what other purpose would we be here? We are in harmony." And so the People did gather around the Great One, hearing his words, hearing the statement of purpose, feeling the wisdom of his entreaties, lest they forget who they are. And yet, first one and then another felt great compassion rise from within their hearts.

One young man spoke. "Oh Great One, we feel compassion for those who have forgotten. Can't we go and gather them," then turning toward the People, "that they too might join us at the time of the full Moon Mother?"

Even as the brave one spoke, others also felt compassion for the People who had forgotten. The same thought, the same feelings, the same question rose within them. "Can't we go forth and gather them?" They spoke amongst themselves. "Then when we walk the truths they will see the light emanating. Perhaps they would remember!" They all turned toward the Great One, waiting upon his words.

He was proud of them. They had responded with courage. "Oh Great People," he spoke, "this then is the second purpose: that we go forth and be a light unto them and gather them together. For here amongst us our numbers are few, yet there are scores upon this Mother." Standing, reaching his arms outward, he resounded the call. "Hear ye, all People! The new beginning, the new day is upon you!" As if from a great canyon the words rumbled. "Feel your being! Resound the truth! Know who you are! Gather together!" His piercing eyes flashed at those about him. He whispered, "Yes, dear ones, yes."

They felt their hearts respond to the second purpose. As if in a vision they saw the numbers grow at the Gathering of the full Moon Mother. They saw the multitudes walking in the light, emanating, placing their feet upon the Mother, walking the truths. The vision was great. They did allow the purpose to fill their entire beings.

And yet there was one feeling a thought take form within himself. He allowed the form to take presence. "Oh Great One, hear these words in honor of your being. How would we go forth and yet remember who we are? For you have said that the others have forgotten." He stepped closer. "How would we go forth and remember, that we might be the gatherers and not be lost as the rest?" He motioned toward the trees. "Beyond this expanse resides great confusion! We feel it. How can we remember what the others could not? Speak, oh Great One, that this might truly be the new beginning and not another end!"

The People felt the rippling of the question amongst themselves. They felt it flow within them. And there birthed once again the asking of guidance. They looked for the answers upon the face of the Great One. Shaking his head he said, "Oh great people, even as you are, you change. Hear these words: You are the truth! You are the very light itself! And yet you ask!" Looking from one face to another, he saw that his words shook them. "Can you feel the change that has come upon you even as the mere thought of confusion has come to you? Feel this amongst you? Feel you?"

His words pleaded with them to see and understand what had just occurred. They had felt the confusion of the multitudes, for it was their way that each share the thoughts and feelings of all the others. They had felt it fill them: the multitudes' frantic asking became their asking. For that moment they had forgotten. It had happened so quickly.

He spoke gently. "Remember the patterns. Remember walking in the light. Remember the darkness and the light." He soothed them. "Reside in the truths, for you are the ones who walk the truths so that they might live upon this Great Mother."

And with the Great One's beseeching, the light amongst the People rekindled. Wide-eyed, they looked at each other, knowing what was beyond: the terrible confusion. Now they knew well of those who had forgotten. They felt the strength of the light return. They remembered. Then this was the first lesson upon the Great Mother. Glowing once again, they turned to the Great One. He knew they needed more time before they went beyond. "Stay only amongst yourselves," he said, "until next we meet." He instructed them to remain in the field and in the area around the trees for one month. "Then we will meet again and speak again." Even with these last words, his body returned to essence.

For a few moments longer they remained transfixed at the place where he had been, and then they turned away. The holding place where they would live for the next thirty days called to them. Some walked around the field filled with flowers, others to the tall green trees, and a few to the riverbank. It was pleasant here, the gifts were bountiful.

At the edge of the field, one came upon a patch of red earth. He squatted down to examine it more closely, scooping a little in his hand to feel the texture. It was cool and moist and stained his fingers. With two fingers, he drew lines around the edge of his face and joined them with a V upon his forehead, the symbol of the opening bud. He felt the truth of the symbol in his being. In this manner, he took it upon himself to be the bearer and caretaker of that one truth. Lest they forget.

One young woman climbed upon the great rocks and there she discovered a tiny shaded niche. Her curious poking finger felt something. She moved it around a little more and then brought it to the light. Upon her finger was a soft, fine, blue powder. She drew a line around her face, from one temple to another, and connected it with a large V across each cheek, a blue symbol upon her. She would carry its truth. She would be it: the bud nearly a blossom. Lest they forget.

And yet another, as she lay in the tall grasses, felt drops of liquid falling upon her. One leaf contained a tiny puddle of gold. She dipped her fingers in the warm liquid and drew a line around her face, from one temple to another. She connected them with a long line down to her chin and back. Golden lines upon her so that she might become the truth itself: the open blossom. She became the bearer of that truth. Lest they forget.

The sound of moving waters called the two explorers. There on the river-bank, they both found their own treasures. He, thick brown clay, and she, a tiny round ball amongst the pebbles. His hands dug into the cool, sticky stuff. Upon his body he drew a circle, and within the circle a cross. She opened the ball and within sparkled white luminescent powder. With one finger she gathered the powder and drew two circles: one on her forehead and one on her chin. Within the circles she drew curved spokes. Two quick movements joined the circles with two lines running straight down the middle of her face. The two explorers each became the embodiment of their truths.

Some drew an entire pattern, while others only a small part of a pattern. Upon one arm went three blue waving lines, upon a foot the head of an arrow with one line trailing back, and upon one hand was drawn a red ball. When the last one had placed a symbol on his being, they returned to the field and joined in the circle. The lighted patterns in the center began pulsating again, flashing through the approaching darkness. And they do simply be who they are: the People maintaining the truths.

Thus are the truths of the story of the first day of the People upon the Great Mother. At the beginning of the darkness, they formed their cocoons, weaving within them the pattern they had drawn upon themselves. And through the darkness the truths do radiate from each cocoon and from the center. The universe watches.

CHAPTER TWO

The Hearing of the Call

Planet Earth, a village nestled within the base of a mountain

It was at the very beginning of the day that their leader spoke with them. Sleep had barely left their bodies and he was calling them together for a meeting. What could be so important?

"While you were sleeping the Ancient One called me to the top of this mountain," he began, even as some were still stepping from their huts. They saw him point to the mountain behind their community and hurried to hear his words.

"The Ancient One spoke with me. The new time is here. A new beginning is here. Oh wonderful friends," his hand grasped at the air in front of him, "our people have come for us!" Never before had they seen him so excited! What did he mean? What people?

"I've seen the patterns in the sky — both in the day and at night! He pointed to one they all knew. "Patterns which you, weaving woman, weave in your blankets." His eyes searched for another and he pointed again. "Patterns which you, warrior, paint upon your brow! Patterns which we place upon our pottery! Patterns which we draw upon our skins! I have seen these same patterns lighted in the sky!"

He walked amongst them, touching one brightly colored shawl and tugging at the leggings of a small boy in his mother's arms. "We've been carrying these patterns with us, even placing them on our children's clothing! What are these patterns? Where did they come from?"

They looked around at each other wondering if anyone knew. No one responded. "Do you remember when we first came into your village?" Some nodded. Yes, there were a few. "And yet, on this day I have been to the top of the mountain and there the Ancient One spoke with me and rekindled in me those memories."

He leapt up on the rock behind him and yelled out down to the end of the well-worn path to the dwellings, "Here! Come here! Bring those children here.

Set aside your working! Set aside your hunting! Set aside your playing! Come here!" He waited until the entire village was gathered and seated on the grass around him. "Now hear these words: There was a day," he began, "when we felt the living force flowing in us. We were only a few," he said, pointing to his fingers. "You could count us on four hands." He spoke of a time before he and his compatriots had come to their village. It was strange to their ears. "There we were in the cave," he said, drawing a curved line across the sky. "The light of violet crystalline structures maintained us." His eyes sparkled as he spoke. "There came a time when we felt the life force again and we gathered, standing in the great crystal cave."

They whispered to each other and he answered, "Why haven't we told you this story before? Because we had forgotten!" Before they could speak amongst themselves again, he continued, "We traveled through long caverns until we saw the light of day. There stood the Great One at the door. Greeting us, beckoning us forth. And we came. We felt the Great Wind Spirit blow upon our being. We felt the light upon us. We breathed once again.

"The Great One spoke with us, beseeching us to remember who we were. And we did...for a time." Tears formed in his eyes. "As we walked the plains, we felt the presence of others. And when we came upon them, they looked at us in wonder, for the brilliance of our light spoke to them. They called us Great Ones, as you have called me Great One.

"The feeling of the People reaching out, called to us, each of us. And we responded and came amongst them, amongst you, dear ones...amongst you." He motioned to their village. "You had created a place here and we recognized some of your patterns. And then after a while, we began to forget who we were.

"It was slow in occurring. We didn't even recognize it until one day, one day we awakened at dawn and we had forgotten — everything! We only knew we were your Great Ones!"

He looked about, pausing to gaze upon one and then another. "And here we have lived with you, dear ones. We have grown in number. Many of you gathered here have come from afar. Why did you come?" He paused a moment. "You came because there is union here. Here we are in union with each other!" Their smiles confirmed his words. "Yes, here you have come and we have created much together. And yet beneath it all is great emptiness, for we have forgotten." He asked again, "Why did you come to us? Because the very essence of our being resonated with you! Yes, we say to you now, we are the People. We came amongst you and long ago you did the same. You came to others and others came to others. We have all forgotten...."

He pointed to himself. "This is the day of memory for this one of the People. Yes! The time is at hand." They strained to understand. He continued, "Once again, there has been the calling of the People and from the great bowels of Earth they have come. They gather! I have seen their lights! I have seen the patterns in the sky! I have seen it!"

Never before had they heard their Great One speak like this. Some wondered what had happened atop their mountain to make him speak so, and others strained still more to understand. It was as if they had perhaps dreamed what he was saying.

"Why have I called you to gather here like this? That you might hear. Perhaps memories will begin to rekindle within you...memories of who you are." He spoke calmly to them, placing his hand on the shoulder of one, holding the hand of another, stilling their anxieties at his strange way of being.

"See these patterns upon your being, upon your skin, upon your own heart, upon your sleeping blanket – upon your very own sleeping blanket?" They couldn't deny that they really didn't know why they drew the patterns. It was just that their old ones had taught them.

"Yes, dear ones, I know you cannot remember. That is why we are gathered here today." He stood, towering over them. "I will emanate the light so that you might begin to remember. As the Ancient One spoke to me, I speak to you. Are you ready?"

They looked to one another, whispering, "What is he going to do, this Great One? What is he going to do?"

Before they could utter another sound he stretched his arms out wide. "Then I give to you this light that you might see the golden light of that which you are."

Before their eyes he began to glow. A little at first and then not only around him but in him and through him, a great golden light shone. It grew and grew. Golden patterns – their patterns – radiated from his being and reflected onto them. The power of his words fell upon them. "Hear you the truths! See you the truths! Here you witness yourself! Know who you are!"

Many of the People fell upon their faces, covering their heads with their hands, for the light of their Great One nearly blinded them. Others stood in awe at the transformation of their Old One into this Being of Light, the strength of truth. They felt it flowing and yet they could only stand in awe. Others wept, wept only for the occurrence, so grand was it. And yet others, but a few, began feeling within themselves a flowing, began feeling a knowing...a knowing! And even as they looked at their own limbs, they began to see light. They stood, the light emanating from their beings. Their remembrance was kindled again. They gazed upon the Great One, their Old One, and in their gaze, they received the strength.

Still others, friends and family of these lighted ones, did begin to reach forward in fear, in fear of losing them! The light was so bright that they shielded their own eyes and turned away. And one who turned away was a young woman who had a bent leg from a fall atop the mountain. She turned away, curling herself upon the Earth in hiding. And she felt upon her shoulder...at first she daren't look. What would that be, touching her shoulder? And then she did feel the flowing within her, the life force. Still she tried to move, to crawl away. And yet the life force filled her and soon the flowing was greater than her fear, and she turned to see. It was her friend, one who had become the light, and it was his hand that was on her shoulder. Yes. He was reaching to her. Gathering her hands, he pulled her upward. When her eyes met his, the flowing began between the two of them and her body became filled with the light. Her leg was straightened. She stood! Glowing patterns flowed between them. And that which she had been, huddled on the ground, did pass from her. Newness arrived and from deep within came remembrance of who she was: the People. Still there were those who ran.

Still there were those who grabbed their staffs and fled into the hills. One young mother scooped up her child and pressed him tightly to her as she raced away. And yet those tiny eyes did peer over her shoulder and see the lighted ones, and without her knowing, the child began to glow. Even though they did flee, that little one carried the light with them. The small number of those who remained gathered together and formed a circle. The light from their Great One filled them. They felt the truths moving in the depths of their being. They became the truths. They remembered. In this manner they remained for three days and three nights, radiating the truths.

Then on the fourth day, their old one, his limbs strong, beckoned them. "Come to the Gathering. Come, the Ancient One has shown me the way." Before them, he waved his arm in a great circle and created a hovel of light. It was the exact form of their huts, only it was made of light. It was a hovel into which those who had remained might enter, if they would dare. He turned to those still hiding behind the bushes, those in the trees, those behind the caves, and said to them, "You hide from your own selves, dear ones. Enter this hovel. Know who you are. And then come. We are the same." And then he turned and, with the others, began the journey, for the Ancient One had shown him the way. They departed from the encampment, and as they placed their feet upon the Great Mother, they felt the newness of their beings. They felt the strength of their beings. They were one.

Location: Planet Earth, the Great Hall within the King's Castle

"Bring those children. All of you come here," he bellowed his orders. He had been sitting all morning, sitting up there on the dynasty's golden throne. It was his, the throne with its carved dragons, the palace — its grandness and splendor had easily become his home — the servants, always bowing, always in awe, and always whispering once his back was turned, and his people in the village below. It was all his.

He had tried again and again simply to be their friend, to stop their continual bowing, but they had placed him above them from the very start. The spiritual tablets had described him exactly, they had said, and so from the first moment they saw him, they called him King and bowed. Only the children, when he could scoop them away from their unsuspecting parents, would allow him to laugh and play and carry on as one of them. "All of you!" They were always delighted to be included in any activity with their beloved king, and gladly they came running when they heard his call.

His voice echoed through the main hall. "Friends who call yourselves servants! All of the servants! Come!" He leaned forward a little, looking down from the tiered rise. "Set aside your things. Come here!" The rustling of clothes and the hurried padding of feet upon tiles ushered them in. They all placed their hands together and bowed before him. Lowering their gazes and standing perfectly still, they waited to hear what he would say.

"This day, I have had a dream." He banged his fist on the dragon's head. "Please! Just this once, look at me! Place your eyes on me!" They followed his order. Hesitantly, they looked up at him.

"I had a dream that I would make a great journey to the North. In the dream, you came. Yes! In the dream, you came with me." He waved his arm at them. "Not as you are. Not as you are."

Stepping down two steps to the first landing, he sat casually. Perhaps that was one of the reasons they loved him — he had broken so many of the old rules. It was rumored that once he had even called the children to come and play on the very throne itself while he laughed and told them delightful stories. And still he could not get them to stop bowing before him.

"In this ear," he continued, "I have had the whisperings. Over and over I have heard the words, 'Remember, Remember.' I have even placed this great hand upon this great ear to stop the whisperings. And yet, they did not stop.

"Then the dream became clear. Hear you these words, for year after year after year, we have been sitting here." (All the kings referred to themselves as "we," they had told him, and he had become so accustomed to their ways that even now he automatically called himself "we.") He pointed to the throne and then down to the floor where they stood. "And you have been bowing and kneeling there. Since the day that we came into your presence, you placed us here and here we did gladly sit, and you did serve. Great honor you did bestow upon us. From this mouth, you did hear the words, 'we are the same,' yet you have continued to bow at our feet, in deepness of honor.

"And yet the dream has come. Then on the morrow, we would leave your presence." They stirred a little, wondering where he would go and why he was leaving. "There are those of you who will come." He stepped down to the next landing as he spoke. "All may come! But there are those who will choose to remain. You are free to choose."

He felt their fear and confusion. They didn't understand what he was saying, and still he continued, even though what he had to share with them was beyond words. "Before you choose, we will reveal ourselves to you, that you might know who you are. All may come. 'Tis your choice now. When we first came here, our purpose was to gather you and rekindle in you the remembrance. And yet when you saw us, you fell upon your knees. Remember?" A few moved back as he stepped down to the first landing, the closest he had been to some of them. "We told you to rise, but there you stayed!"

He placed his hands together and lowered his head to them. "We honor you. For you have honored us." On his knees, he bent his body low and touched his forehead to the landing. "We bow to you, for you have bowed to us."

Before they could turn away, he stood. His loud words held them. "And hear ye these words: The day of this is over. The day of bowing is over!" He paused only a moment for the words to settle in them. "Then we reveal ourselves to you, that you might know yourselves." Tears had already begun to fall upon the cheeks of those who knew him well, of those he had coaxed to come close. What was he going to do? What did all this mean? "And then we will begin, for there is a great journey that we will take together. Yet some will stay; even though you have professed your love, you still will remain. 'Tis your choice now. Free you have always been, and free you are this day.

"Bowing will not bring you this light. It is within you. And when we reveal ourselves, then perhaps you will reveal yourselves." He outstretched his arms before them. His words rumbled through the very foundation of the palace. "Prepare yourself for the awakening, for it is at hand!"

Not only did their king stand and radiate the greatest light they had ever seen, he stepped down and dared walk amongst them. The splendor of it all pushed them to their knees, yet he motioned them up again. They felt the glow of his being. As he walked amongst them, he caressed one face, kissed one forehead, and pulled them up until all were standing.

Before they could clear their whirling minds, he pushed the great doors open and out he walked. They watched him go. He turned once and beckoned them to come, to follow, to walk with him on the great journey. Waving his arm, he beckoned them with his being. There were those who felt the call, the decision to go. And with the first step, they did radiate light. First one, then another, then another...with each first step they began to radiate light. And he remained turned, standing there, beckoning them. Soon nearly all had taken the first step.

But a few remained. One weeping on the golden throne, weeping. Yet another gathering some jewels in his pockets, to flee with the treasures. And yet others, hiding in the darkness.

And even as they followed behind, the numbers of three hands and three hands, he turned again and into the darkness of the great palace he breathed the word, "Remember." And the word in his breath filled the great halls.

Then he stepped forward in the strength of his being, in the light of his being. And those beings did follow. They began their journey to the North. Light beings, emanating light. And yet his body a beacon still, with every step, they became brighter and brighter. It was as if they were a line of light, winding up the great hills to the North.

And in the village below, the People saw the line of light moving up to the mountain. And there, one being, a young boy traveling, saw the line of light. He felt a tingling. Without another thought, he dropped everything. He ran, ran through the village, out from the village, up toward the great palace. Running. Running, until he could see where they had stepped. For where they had stepped on the great Mother Earth, there were prints of light. The boy placed his tiny foot in the prints of light and he, too, began to glow. He continued onward, for he would catch them, he thought. "Where they are going, I will go."

And their journey began, even unto the last.

It appeared that different locations bore the same occurrence. One here and another there. The great teachers heard the call. And even in their turning and calling to those who had been serving them and to those who had studied with them, the numbers increased. Some heard the call. Some did come.

At the sea, there was one teacher so great and grand, speaking the truths.

It was in his private quarters that he allowed himself to speak his true feelings. Sitting in his chair and gazing out past the stone walls to the sea, his beloved sea, the grand teacher spoke aloud, as if to an invisible companion. "Why am I so alone in this? Of all the students who come to me, there isn't one who can think for himself!" He pounded his fist on the arm of the chair. "Where are my compatriots? Where are those who can think? Where have they gone?"

The stone walls, grey and bulky, refused to answer. His memories answered, as they always had, with melancholic pictures. "Did we not meet at the café often, speaking together, excited in our ideas?" Breathing a deep sigh, he leaned his head back on the chair. "Yes, we did. Then she did go her way and he went his way, each seeking that success, that golden apple that they might pluck for themselves. Of course they would!" He remembered his dear friends well. "Success," he hissed. He reflected for a moment. "And yes, I too sought success, teaching in this grand hall, seemingly for centuries."

He stood and lumbered his great body to the window. Shaking his fist at the sea he cried out, "I am hungry for compatriots! I am thirsty for speaking with someone who can think! Where are you!"

Turning back to the papers on his writing table, he fingered a few pages. "These children who pretend to be men write down my words on paper. They actually write down my words!" Pushing back long grey hair, he groaned to himself, "What am I doing here? What have I done? I have fooled myself!"

Long strides carried him back and forth from one wall to another. "I have fooled myself," he repeated under his breath. "Thinking of the grandness of position, and wanting – yes, wanting – to share those truths." He stopped short. "I hardly remember what they are. The truths!"

He pulled papers from the dresser drawer. Fumbling through the stack, he chuckled to himself, "Maybe *I* wrote them on paper somewhere, trying to translate them that these young ones could understand them. They could not hear the words. They could not see the light." He paused in his search. "The light, yes, the light...that light."

He pushed the papers back into the drawer. "But it is all merely memories, memories." Rubbing his worn hands together seemed to help him think. "Perhaps I will take a vacation. Go away from the sea." Even as he said the words, his heart ached at the futility of the just-made plans. He pressed his pounding forehead against the cool glass and then flung open the windows. "If it were not for this beloved sea, I would have perished long ago. It is she that nourishes me, the sea." He breathed in her salty perfume. "Blessed are you, the sea, you give me life!" But today even the sea couldn't still his discontent.

"What has become of me? What has become of me? The teachings...." He dragged himself back to his chair and slumped down into its worn softness. He seemed to drift off for a while, and an onlooker might have falsely judged his intent listening to be dozing. The words had come to him. And then, with firm resolve, he smacked his lips as he always did when he had made a decision and announced, "This I will do. This I will do!"

The young boy who had come for his usual lessons had heard his teacher's words. He paused a little outside the door, not to eavesdrop, but to give his beloved teacher the privacy of his own words. Now the words called to him!

"Come here, garçon, come here!" When the boy timidly entered the room, there was his teacher thrashing through things. "This day there will be no classes and on the morrow, no classes will be held. Come here, bring that satchel. I will gather a few things together."

The boy began to gather his teacher's traveling desk, only to be stopped with, "No! No! No writing papers, no. We will not write another word."

He responded to the unspoken words of his favorite student. "Ah, you would ask where I am going. Upon the dawning of this day, I had not one inkling, not one thought...and yet at this moment, I feel within myself a calling. Yet it is true, I do not know where I am going!"

He muttered to himself, "Just a few things, what shall I take?"

The boy gathered the usual traveling papers, but before he could tie them together, his teacher pulled them from his hand. "A letter saying who I am? I am who I am! I do not need letters saying who I am."

He saw the boy looking at the money bag, "A few coins? A few coins have ruined me! No more!" He cast the bag across the room. "Don't you have them. They will ruin you also, those few coins in your pocket."

He smoothed his clothing, "I will simply go as I am." Again reading the boy's thoughts he said, "No, I am not too old for this. I have more life force flowing in me than you could dream of in your deepest dreams, young one!"

Turning away, the boy tried to hide his hurt. "Come here, I am not angry with you." His teacher's voice had softened. "Come here." His large hand gently pulled the boy's chin upward. "You see this being before you? Yes. I have deep love for you."

And even as he spoke, his eyes glazed a little. "There is a calling, there is a calling. I feel it inside me." He pulled the boy to him. "You, amongst all of the others, have known me as I am, known me when the torment of my mind has taken me, known me when the rages have taken me, yes. Yes, Yes, Yes," he stroked the boy's head, "and you know me when I speak of the truths. Yes you do." He smiled. "And you have never written them down!" Bending down a little, he looked the boy directly in the eyes. "For this, I do praise you!"

He slipped the satchel strap over his shoulder. "I will walk along the shore amongst the rocks, and the cliff will not claim me. I will walk light-footed along the way. And from there...I don't know. Yet, yet I had not a thought that I would be doing this, this day."

He looked about his room, a quick glance here and there, and then said, "No, I doubt that I would return. Blessing that it is. Blessing!"

And the great teacher began walking to the door. And even as he opened it, he felt strength. It was as if the light washed upon him, as if the past and the present were one. The memories, the dreams, the teachings, the classes and the students flashed before his eyes. He saw them as if they were being washed from him by the light, by the wind rushing in upon him. And his spirit was cleansed.

Just as he stepped from the portal to the Earth, he turned back to see that young one, the one he did love so, and there he was, his young body standing there glowing with a strange golden light.

The teacher smiled to himself and looked back to say, "I suppose this means you are coming with me!"

And together, the two began the journey. Their strength increased as they walked away from the building, away from the classes and toward the cliffs. And when the old teacher reached for a walking staff, the young one assisted him. And when they touched hands, there was a tingling between them. Something was happening between them! They didn't know exactly what it was, but it drove them onward with great purpose. And still they didn't know where they were going or exactly what route they would take. It just drove them onward.

The crashing sea below thundered in their ears as they reached the top of the great cliffs. On the green grass they rested, sitting across from each other. When the young boy looked at his hands, in the center was a light. It looked almost like symbols flashing at him! He thought it was quite curious and wanted to be assured that what he was seeing was actually true. He turned his hand and faced it toward the old teacher. "Do you see anything here," he began, and yet, when he looked up, the teacher's face was filled with golden light. His eyes were closed as if he were in a trance. The light from his palm beamed to the forehead of the teacher. And there, in the center, the patterns formed once again.

He wondered how long they had been sitting, when he placed his hand downward again. He looked at the old one, his teacher, sitting there with his legs crossed. "His back is so straight," he thought. "You look so fine, my dear teacher!"

Then the teacher opened his mouth, and great, deep, resonant sounds came forth from the bowels of his being. It was as if the wind had rushed from inside to without. The sounds echoed across the cliffs. And then again, the sounds came from the very depths of the teacher. Building and building, they continued. He outstretched his arms and stood.

He was filled with radiating light. He spoke words the lad had never heard before. "Ahh-klaa-eee-khlee!" The words flowed from him, "Ahh-klaa-eee-khlee." Three times again he said the words. As they came forth from his lips, it was as if the letters formed patterns in the air. Patterns, ahh-klaa-eee-khlee, as if they hung there for a moment, and then dispersed.

The boy, still gazing, had no thoughts in his mind, for the regular way of thinking had left him. He was as he was, pure light. He felt the resonating sounds enter his being. He heard the sounds come from his own being. Yes, he too was saying the words.

Pointing his finger at the old one, he repeated over and over, "You are the People! You are the People. You are the People." He wondered at what he was saying.

Then the old one sat across from him again, and he took his finger and drew in the earth the symbols once again. First one, then another. And as he completed one, it radiated with light. And then another, radiating with light. And upon the lad's face, he could see the reflection of the patterns, even though it was the light of day.

"I am not alone," the teacher thought in the back of his mind. Even as he was drawing the symbols, he thought, "I am not alone. He is one also." Memories flooded him. Golden beings, gathered together in the field, walking together, radiating the light. And even in the strength of his being, he wept, allowing his weeping to wash away the last remembrance of loneliness, the last desire to be together, washed away. For then he knew who he was — the People.

He said to his beloved lad, "The People are here again! They have come for us!"

Yes, in many different locations on the Great Mother were those who began to remember, were those who were filled with light. For in the great golden field surrounded by trees erect as they, under the sky so blue under which they traveled, were the People. The People, in the light of day, in the dark of night, radiated the truths, for it was the first purpose that they remember who they were.

And they did partake of the fruits of the Earth. Red berries here, fruits of every kind came from the bushes and the trees. And they were nourished. Soon even the bushes glowed with light.

They continued in the same manner with only one exception. During the day, one woman began to weave a great, large cocoon at the edge of the field. Then another began also, and soon they filled the perimeter with large, blue cocoons, large enough to hold two or three.

When night came, as was their usual way, they created their own cocoons and entered them. They all glowed, the large blue and the small white, essence lighting the dark. Thusly they maintained themselves, until the fullness of the Moon Mother. Then the Great One would speak again.

And the call resounded throughout the universe, "Gather together! Come ye here, oh great People. Come ye here. We are the People. Once again we come for you."

As ones traveled from here and there, from every location, there were those who saw and felt the call, and even as they walked through little villages, there were those who joined them. Sometimes one, sometimes as many as one hand. And the Gathering began. The call was heard.

Blessed are you who hear the telling of this tale.

CHAPTER THREE

The Observers

Location: Universe, Observation Room

The bank of monitors showed him just the pictures he was looking for. The old man leaned forward for a closer examination. "They seem to be doing quite well, don't they? Maintaining everything quite well." He turned a quick glance to the technician. "Interesting planet, isn't it?" They smiled to each other and then at the screens.

"It is the planet of incubation and everything is according to schedule. Everything." He spoke with satisfaction, as if the project were his own. "All the reports that have come to us have been quite pleasing. And, and, and the program has actually worked, hasn't it?"

"It appears to be working, sir."

"If they can maintain those symbols...."

It was his usual way, to become so completely and utterly involved. Yet this project in particular required all of their complete and undivided attention. He could hardly contain his warm pride. "Have you seen the calls? The calls for the Gathering have gone out and they're responding! They're coming!"

"Switch to another screen," he motioned. "Let's see them." The technician adjusted a few dials and brought in a closeup of the great mountain and the place where the leader had spoken with his people. The spot was still glowing with light, and the old man liked the confirming evidence. "Ah, yes." He began to lean back and then jerked forward. "What is that over there? Over there," his finger pointed.

They both peered at the screen. "Yes sir," confirmed the technician, "there's something there all right." He adjusted more dials until they could see a full view of a steady, pulsating light in the clearing. "I don't recognize it, sir, do you know...?"

The old man slapped his leg, "Why it's a hovel!" He repeated under his breath, "One of them has erected a hovel." He hurriedly adjusted some of the dials himself. "Must have been his own idea. We don't have anything like that in our plans."

The technician flipped through his reference book and found the information on the hovel. "Now I know why I didn't recognize it." His finger underlined the words as he read the description aloud: "A holding structure for the purpose of initiating transformation and either (1) providing a supporting atmosphere until the occupant is able to maintain the new vibration or (2) holding the occupant until further assistance arrives by physical or telepathic means."

"Yep, that's what it is," confirmed the old man.

"But sir, it says here it's *experimental.*"

"We never did put it into use," he chuckled, "until now." He had a reputation for adventure and the unexpected — and dependability. Only in this past decade had he consented to joining the Council, even though they had approached him many years before, and at times he still yearned for the excitement of dimensional travel.

He rubbed his chin. "There's bound to be someone who'll go in there. You'd better keep your eye on it."

"But sir," the technician was still reading, "there's no authorization date. And who's going to assist?"

"We'll just have to keep a close watch and when the time comes for the Gathering, then we'll see how many have entered and how far along they've come."

He motioned for his friend to take a closer look. "Do you see any patterns in there?"

"No, sir." He switched on the inside viewer. "None at all."

"Good. Then it's just a hovel he built." They both nodded in agreement. "Quite bright though, isn't it? Quite bright." For a moment, he let his thoughts carry him to the time when he and his friend had begun research on the possibility of interdimensional use of hovels. "Yes...."

Then, switching topics, he said, "What about within? Let's look inside the planet. Can we get that on the screen?" He lovingly slapped the young technician on the back. "Let's take a look."

Different levels within the planet Earth appeared on the screen. Each level radiated its own particular color. The technician, an expert in his field of remote viewing, telepathically called the caverns and tables of sleeping beings into view.

The steady, uninterrupted flow of color gave him the information he was looking for. "This level maintained quite well."

"Yes, sir, we've been quite happy with the results."

"However," continued the old man, "visually this gives us nothing, you know. You see the levels, you see the lights. It really doesn't tell us how they are maintaining."

"It's a matter of developing a sensitivity to the psychic waves, sir, and there are varying degrees of color. This closeup should demonstrate what I mean." With one simple adjustment he brought in a detailed picture of one of the tables holding a sleeping being.

The old man's face showed approval of his agility and precise maneuvering. "Yes, I know." Even though it wasn't his field, he read the colors accurately. "I know there are subtleties that are read, but..."

"I do know what you mean, sir," the young man interrupted. "All in all, we can be so backward at times!" They both knew that this equipment was the most advanced they had ever used. It was a good joke and their rolling laughter filled the observation room.

"It's nearly time for Council," said the old man, catching his breath. "We can see these other levels later. Let's go to the Council."

"One moment, sir! What is that?"

"What..."

"Level Three. Level Three!"

They both peered at the varying colors surrounding the beings on Level Three. The old man spoke first. "Seems to be some activity there, doesn't there?"

"Definitely, sir. Definitely!"

"Could it be the call — felt even at Level Three?" The old man waved his arm. "Tell the Council to hold off. We'll view this a little longer."

While the technician placed the call, the old man adjusted the pictures by hand. "Level Three. Green. Let's see if·we can get a little closer...there." He saw the varying colors. "It's true! It is true!"

The technician returned just in time to respond to the orders. "When did they begin? Check that, when did all this begin?" Even before he finished speaking, figures flashed on the screen. "Oh, that's good, it's not so advanced. He rubbed his chin again. "Level Three, green. They'll be ready soon. They're assimilating even as we speak!"

"But sir, that does bring the schedule closer."

The old man's gestures interrupted. "Look at them! Green. Green. Yes, they are wonderful!" His loving smile stilled the growing concern of the young technician. "It'll be a little while." They both knew this was a first, yet let the words remain unspoken. "What will be will be," the old man whispered.

He allowed a brief pause to settle between them. Then he said, "Check Four. Let's have a look at Level Four, orange." New pictures appeared for his examination. "Humm...no activity at all." He moved from one screen to another, "There, the bowels are still clear and the great depths, see...yes, yes, they're still in slumber. Good. Ahh, yes."

Tossing down his notes he said, "Well then, now we'll go to Council."

Before his young prodigy could shut off the monitors, the old man leaned forward for a quick re-examination. "All in all, they're doing quite well at maintaining, this time. Perhaps," he sighed deeply, "perhaps this time it will really happen. Strong, they're strong in their purpose." He succumbed to one last look at the first monitor. "And there are those who are coming, see? See here, look at this one. They're coming!"

"We'll see." He pulled himself from the screens. "Let's go to Council."

The Council Meeting

The leader of the Council opened in the usual manner. She had been their leader throughout this last phase. Her long golden hair was pulled up and tied atop her head, as was the custom for all leaders, both men and women. Her flowing white robe bore the familiar gold emblem and, following tradition, she touched it as she began. "This Council is resumed."

Her familiar smooth, clear words continued, "This is the first gathering of the Council since the beginning of Purpose One. And now we would like to hear how our loving Mother Planet is doing." All eyes around the white oval table turn to the old man. He and the technician had been the last ones to hurry into the meeting, and they all anxiously awaited his news.

"Purpose One is maintaining with the originators. The call is very strong. Many are responding." Even though he calmly spoke of the recent viewings, a slight twinkle danced in his eyes. "There are but a few unexpected events, as is usual on this Mother Planet. Our beacons are at the maximum for what they would be able to receive at this time."

One councilman around the table spotted the twinkle. "There is something that you are not saying, isn't there! Something quite unusual! Even though you have said the unusual is usual on this Mother Planet, speak please, dear brother, of the unusual. We are eager to hear, for there is deep love and joy in this heart, for the People, that they are maintaining."

Another man, glowing the green color-code of his level, interrupted, "I can speak of what it is." He could barely contain himself with the exciting news, "We have activity on Level Three! Green. Activity! Two levels below that which was activated to start. Two levels below!"

He motioned to them all. "Now you know the strength of the call. It seems perhaps we have underestimated the People." A tear slipped from the corner of his eye. "Yes! This heart is filled with joy."

He turned to old man. "Isn't it true? For we are of Level Three and when there is assimilation on Level Three, we feel it. The essence of our being is changed, of course. It has been coming. Even I, until just before this gathering, didn't recognize exactly what was occurring. Lying dormant for eons, isn't it true?" He realized he had spoken out of turn and explained, "I spoke first so that I would be assured that my readings of self were correct. Speak brother, speak."

The old man confirmed the news. "Yes, yes it is true. There is activity on Level Three. They are assimilating." He could no longer contain his broad smile. "This is going to be quite a Gathering!" He turned to the representative of Level Three. "They'll need some assistance after the initial assimilation. Of course, you know this. They can't maintain on their own at that level. Are your people ready to begin transmitting to them?"

He nodded, and the old man approved. "Good. Good."

The leader of the Council continued the questioning. "Level Two of blue, have you no activity at all?" The blue-glowing representative of Level Two shook his head and replied, "Nothing."

"All the others?" she questioned. Level representatives around the table signaled no activity. "Even unto the core?" They signaled no again. "Fine, fine."

"It appears that in this Gathering the entire Mother Planet might attend. There is a great call, and the activity on Level Three does point to that...." Her words trailed off. "Then, my dear brother," she said, turning to the old man, "are there any other unusual occurrences that you are withholding from us? Yes," she conceded, "lovingly withholding from us?"

Her smile spread across the table to him. "Then speak, if there is one other little surprise. We feel the ripples of your great humor amongst us, dear brother."

He began, "It really is quite insignificant. Yet, one of them has created a hovel. At the beginning, where his transformation took place, he created a hovel. Of course," he chuckled, "we all know who that one is." He remembered his friend. "He said he would be there until the last, and it is like him to create a hovel. Yes, as the progress begins, he is nearly at full capacity of the vibrations with which he came. We are monitoring. Thus far, no one has entered the hovel. However, it is highly likely that at least one, perhaps two or three, will enter. Once one enters then the others will feel the attracting radiation. Truthfully, we have not quite decided what to do about it. It's actually a first." He chuckled again. "That brother! He keeps us activated, doesn't he? It would be good to see him again. That is truly the only other surprise. And we did not keep it from you, we just held it in our heart for a moment longer, loving our dear brother.

"And yes, yes, of course, we are all feeling that the People are maintaining Level One.

"Soon we will be at the point where the last gathering dispersed. If they continue to maintain the vibration of their beings beyond this time, as they carry the symbols, then we are actually entering upon new ground. And then you, Level Two," he pointed to his brother, "might feel some activity. And actually at Level Four! Level Five, of course, well, perhaps we will come to Level Five.

"However, it appears with the activity on Level Three that their transmission is greater than we anticipated. Do you think we should increase our support, especially since the time is approaching when the others dispersed? What do you think? What is your suggestion, sister of mine?"

The leader of the Council spoke. "We are at the maximum — that is, the maximum that we have always given in support of this transformation. Yes, it is true that the signals broke apart with each previous gathering right at this exact point. I am inclined to believe that we could raise a little. However, in raising a little, we might leave a few behind. At this present resonance, even those who have not heard the call still have the opportunity, you see? That is why we have chosen this resonance, as we have agreed previously.

"It is our suggestion that we maintain the level at which we are. And then, as we approach the time of usual dispersement, we'll be ready! Then we can increase, if need be. The increase would actually have to be at the exact moment. Just a little later would cause the ripples we have had in the three previous gatherings. In the meantime, we can all make adjustments in support of our Level Three representatives here so that they can focus directly and completely on the assimilation. Would that be agreed?" Each member affirmed. "Good."

She touched the golden emblem again before stating, "Then we will monitor a little longer. There is still time. When we gather next in Council, then another decision can be made. Perhaps we'll have more information at that time. Until then, we should maintain continually what we have always, lest there be those left behind — in your words, my dear brother."

The old man agreed and added, "We will say one more thing. It is our Gathering that presents itself to the People on the Mother Planet, and those people are ready! They have great compassion for each other. A hovel was created! And every step is lighted! Did you know this? That every step is lighted? Yes, we have been there and we have seen! Even the children of the children are gathering! Even the children of the children."

A ripple of wonder spread throughout the Council. First one and then another allowed the thought pattern to take form; perhaps the union would occur. And then...grandness.

When they had completed their meeting, as was their usual manner, the Council vibrated together, each in his or her own color. Each allowed his/her own sound to come forward and together a great chorus resounded. In this manner they formed a union.

They allowed their light to emanate together, and there was union in light. Then they allowed themselves to disseminate and there was only essence in the Council.

In the very center, the symbols took form and radiated until the last symbol, and there was sound, color and essence together.

Then, where each one had been sitting, golden essence formed and they assimilated themselves. First the golden essence, and then the color they maintained for their own gatherings.

When each had assimilated, they breathed deeply in unison. Without a word, they departed to continue the work that had begun.

The great egg-like room did maintain in slumber, until the Council would meet again.

CHAPTER FOUR

The One Who Remembers

Disseminate: to scatter widely, to spread out.

In this grand universe, there have developed through the dimensions different forces designated for specific purposes. Periodically, a consciousness unites with another or creates a new purpose, empowering that purpose and sending it off, sending it outward.

Thus, in this tale there are those forces presenting themselves periodically. There had been created, at the very beginning of the first gathering upon the Great Mother, a force. The purpose of the force at that time was dissemination. It came, streaking through the universe. The originators of the force of dissemination believed that Mother Earth people had yet another purpose. Initially, they looked with disdain upon the first gathering of the People, even though the purpose of that gathering was to spread a call that all might be one.

The creators of the force of dissemination created their force for the purpose of intercepting the Gathering of the People. Through their stout hearts, they believed that the Earth People should be left on their own.

At the times of gatherings, there comes the moment when the transformation of those coming to the gathering moves from minority to majority. Those creating the force of dissemination also created their force so that it would enter at that precise moment, creating dissemination rather than union: dissemination of form, dissemination of purpose, dissemination of the power of light flowing forth, beckoning the People.

As we speak in this tale, then, we recognize that soon this time will be upon us, moving from minority to majority. Then at that moment, once again, there would come the force of dissemination.

At this particular gathering, however, the force beckoning the People to assimilate has been the most powerful by which the People have ever been beckoned. They came and assimilated themselves, and now they maintain a light, the symbols of their beings, and the time approaches.

So that fear will not destroy their focus of purpose, they have no memory of the approaching force of dissemination. Yet, there is one, one who came two times previous, for the People have been coming to this great Earth Mother, including this time, 1,242,301 times. For eons they have come. And there is this one traveling the Earth who carries the memory of the moment of dissemination. At the moment of dissemination, those who are the People and who are not yet transformed forget who they are. Those who are transformed disseminate.

During the last gathering, at the moment of dissemination, this one being was nearly transformed, but not enough so to be disseminated. He has been traveling the Earth, searching, searching for something. He's not quite clear what...searching...something. All else seems unimportant to him. Searching....

At times he thought he was searching for another like himself. At times he thought that he had almost found another like himself, and yet not really. So he moved onward. One gathering, then another, searching. And yet he knew that if he did find one other like himself, then there would be two who would be still searching, searching for something more.

As he felt the call ripple through his being, it awakened his memories of other times. "What are these times?" he wondered. "Great comrades? Companions? And more? A purpose so grand that it left them beyond concern of anything else? Could these be real memories?"

And yet, at the beckoning of these People, he awakened again and again. The call was so strong that he did once again lift his being for traveling.

And in this traveling, he met two others. He thought, "Who is this old man? Light in his eyes. And that young one with him, innocence and wisdom. They're traveling together," he thought. And yet, they had a purpose beyond all others. They were traveling, too.

He thought that perhaps they three would travel together, and when dusk came, he watched the two, sitting across from each other. They lighted everything! Between them flowed light — between their palms, between their foreheads. It was strong. It was all around them and even floating away from them.

He sat and observed. He knew that light well; it resided within him, but he hadn't called it forward for a very long time. And here were two together, openly radiating! For all to see! Didn't they know it radiated throughout the entire universe? Didn't they know? Perhaps not. He would wait and see. As he sat, he began vibrating and communing with the same light within his own being, and before he knew it, the two, the Old One and the boy, had turned toward him and had faced the palms of their hands toward him.

"Such light! Dare they open so wide?" he thought. "Dare they open so wide!" And then it occurred. The symbols from their hands came to him and he felt the force enter. He felt the force unite with him. He felt himself rejoice! The patterns resounded throughout his being. Every cell of his being manifested the symbols. He was one. Memories and memories flashed before him. At first but a glimpse, and he found his mind trying to catch on to them, those memories. And then they were there! He remembered. He remembered assimilation in the bowels of the Great Earth Mother, he remembered coming forth, he remembered traveling throughout the People, beckoning them, and he remembered the Gathering.

Many were coming together. He was dancing, filled with joy! And then darkness! Separation! Grasping at thick air and nothing there! Darkness so black that he put his fingers to his eyes to feel if they were open; and yet there was nothing to see. Closing his eyes, seeking that communion with the light! The People — where were they? And as he grasped for them and grasped for them, the memory faded and faded...until now.

All these memories flashed before him as the symbols resonated within his being. And then he knew. "The time is at hand," he thought. "It is resounding throughout the universe!" He also remembered the other force, the force of dissemination, like a magnet, the darkness to the light.

And yet the two pulsated, facing themselves toward him, and he dared to open and let the light flow from his being also. And they three were as a great beacon, the greatest of all, for he was the one who remembered. Throughout the universe, the beacon of their light spread. And he expanded himself to fill the entire universe with the knowingness of his being.

And there was near the tree one light. One symbol. One being. And then he knew. It will occur again. The force of dissemination will occur again! "I must get to the Gathering," he thought. "I must get to the Gathering!"

And the two, the old teacher and his young student, the wisdom and the innocence, heard his thoughts, but they still didn't know why. Only the one who remembered knew. And yet they too felt the urgency, even within themselves. They had been feeling it all along.

Upon the great Earth the three traveled together, and in the light of day and the dark of night, they radiated the light, the symbols, the truth.

Their great light spilled into the valleys, into the villages, as they went. There were those who gathered together in the villages, speaking amongst themselves of what was occurring in the mountains.

"Have you seen the light?" they asked each other. "Have you seen the great light on the mountain?"

"Yes," they all nodded in agreement. They had seen it.

"Has anyone seen them this way before?"

There was one who had seen the lights before. He was old. He had seen the lights three times in his lifetime. "Perhaps I am so old," he said, "that perhaps my memory is not so clear, but this does seem to be the brightest of all. It seems to be the brightest. This old feeble mind," he said to them, "still does not remember the lights ever to have been this bright."

They gathered together again in excitement. "Have you heard the Old One? The lights have never been this bright," they said. "Never!"

"Can you see it at night? Can you see it spilling into the village?"

"It's almost like liquid gold," one said.

"Have you been to it?" the other asked.

"No." No one had been to it.

"We are but villagers," one said. "We are not goats! Traveling to the top of the mountain, it would take a goat to go there!"

Then they all laughed together. And yet they looked out their windows at the mountain and waited for the light. And in the darkness, it appeared again! They were transfixed. Soon nearly the entire village was standing awake, looking upward at the mountain. Light. Light spilling forth down the mountainside and nearly right into the village!

Then one said, "You know, I am not afraid!"

And they laughed at him. They laughed. They said, "Of course, it's only light. Who's afraid of light?"

And he said, "Truly, I don't have any fear in me concerning all of this. Have you?"

And they stopped their laughing for a moment, each one thinking about what he had said. First one and then another and then another said, "I have no fear either! There is not one part of fear in me, either!"

Another said, "The only fear I have is thinking of climbing up there!"

And the first said, "I don't even have a fear of that! And I'm not boasting. I just am not afraid. I believe I could do it. Could you?"

And they thought, each of them, some shaking their heads, no, no. Then others really thinking about it.

"Why, I don't have fear of it either," said another.

And then another said, "I've been thinking about it! I've been planning it. I was afraid to say anything. I thought you all might think I had become a little crazy, thought you might try to talk me out of it."

And the first said, "Have you the plans? Would you go? Would you?"

And he thought a moment and said, "I had already decided to go. And since you ask, then I say to you and any others: Who wants to go? For on the morrow, with the first light of day, I'll begin. I have it all planned!"

And another said, "You have it all planned? You even know which way you'll go?"

"Yes," he said. "Come here, I'll tell you."

And they gathered around and he said, as he pointed to the top of the mountain, "You see how the light has been moving each time we see it? It's been moving. I plan to go through the north ridge and up!"

"Why there's no light there," said one. "It's not even there!"

"By the time I get there, the light will be there. It's moving. See for yourself."

And then the first said, "It's a good plan. I'll gather my things. I'll go too, together. 'Tis a good plan, and the north ridge is a comfortable climb."

There were four others, each saying, "I'll come." And they agreed even as their necks stretched upward, looking at the light. It felt as if they could almost drink that light flowing over the edge!

"Looks almost like nectar," one whispered. Yet, no one responded, for they were transfixed by the light.

At the first light of day, six they were as they began, and they knew only that they must see this light first-hand. "They must," they thought. "They must!" And they began.

After the six left, there were those in the village who wished that they had also gone. There were those who shook their heads. There were those who spoke together, speaking of the foolishness. There were those who spoke together, speaking of the bravery. And yet, all, in the darkness, gathered to see where the light was on the mountain.

And the Council? Yes, the Council knew of the force of dissemination, yet they didn't speak of it. Within each one, they knew.

Those who hear this tale, the Council smiles upon you, for they observe your gatherings and say, "They are assimilating." Yes, we speak with you, dear friend, dear reader.

CHAPTER FIVE

Seven Visions

Atop a great mountain, a great Warrior stood, his arms outstretched, reaching. He had received many visions in this very place, visions that he had carried down the mountain, down to his people in the encampment below. At times there were instructions in the visions. At times there were great songs which he taught them and which they then sang in their encampment. At times there was a new symbol and the story of that symbol.

"My people," he thought, "are holy people." Every thing, every way we are, is in honor of everything that is. The rhythm of daily living provided contentment, peace and uplifting visions. Amongst each other, they lived in great peace. "My people are truly great people," he thought.

For in his visions were pictures of other peoples. There were none who lived in peace. And he thought that the Great One had provided these pictures for him that his people might live in peace. Each time the vision came of the conflict, of battles, of fierceness of beings, he thanked the Great One for giving him his people. He thanked the Great One that they lived in peace. And yet, at the sight of the conflict, he had at times wept to see brother battle upon brother. At times in the night he would awaken again and again. The Great One gave him these visions.

He had heard the call. He had felt the beckoning to come to the top of the mountain once again. And he did, traversing to the top, to the holy place. There he stood, reaching outward in great joy and exhilaration. For when he was called, he was filled with the Great One. It was here that they met and spoke together.

"Oh Great One," he spoke, "you have called me here again. Rejoicing am I to be called again."

As in times before, he waited. The Great One would speak with him inside of his being, in his thoughts. He would feel the words enter, trickling in and forming. Then there would be the Great One's words within him. Yet in another time, great pictures would form within his being. And there had been one time when the Great One had taken form and had spoken with him.

This time he wondered, for he knew each was his gift, a gift that he carried to his people below. He spoke with the Great One as if he were speaking with his brother. Then he felt the presence forming around him. He knew the Great One was arriving.

The great deep voice spoke within his being:

"Brother of mine,
Soon the Great Mother shakes herself free.
The village of your people will be no more.
Great Brother,
Gather your people together.
Into the caverns go you."

The First Vision

Before the Warrior's eyes, the Great One showed a vision. There was an entryway, one he had never seen before. It was an entryway through the red rocks to a cavern. With the trees, one could hardly see, and yet there it was. The Great One did see that the Warrior knew.

The Second Vision

Then a second vision did appear. It was a pathway into a large cavern within the Great Mother. And the Warrior saw how his people would travel: this way and then that way, winding around, this way and then that way. He saw. Then the vision was complete.

Then the Great One spoke again, saying,

"These things your people will take:
Holy blanket of sleeping.
That is all. Leave the rest.

"Speak with your people,
They must leave the rest.

"The Great Mother will shake herself free.
Into the cavern go you and the People.

"No food, no skins, nothing will you need.
Everything is provided.

"In three days,
Then you would go.

"For there comes upon this great Earth Mother

A battle that is not a battle,
A battle even in the visions you have not seen.
Great forces come upon this Great Mother,
Great forces.

"Speak with your people,
That they sing the song of love,
Praising the Great Mother.

"All else leave.

"Those who remain behind will perish.
Take the Old Ones with you,
They are needed.
To the cavern,
Go you and your people."

The Warrior was filled and answered, "Blessed are we that your love is so deep that you would send us to the cavern, oh Great One."

His heart sang the Song of Praise to the Great One. Sweetly he sang the Song of Rejoicing. Deeply and resonantly he repeated the Song of Gratitude. And softly he whispered the Song of Holiness.

Then he placed the great feathered headdress upon his being and outstretching his arms, he spoke to the Mother.

"Oh Great Mother,
The Great One has said
Soon you will shake yourself free.

"Oh Great Mother,
He has shown us
Where you will open yourself
That we would enter the cavern.

"Oh Great Mother,
You are our breath,
You are our food,
You are our water,
You are we.

"Oh Great Mother,
Blessed are we, that we walk upon you
And you receive us.

"Oh Great Mother,
Praise be to you!

"Oh Great Mother,
This gift
Opening you to us,
That we might enter,
This gift."

He made the sounds. He danced the dance. He wept the tears. He gathered the Earth in his hands and spread her upon his being, crying, "Oh Great Mother!"

Soon the Wind Spirit came and blew its breath upon the Warrior. And he felt the breath, flowing on his being, blowing within him, breath so deep, filling him. And he breathed deeply.

The Third Vision

And then a spinning white vortex came down upon him and lifted him upward, upward, upward. Soon he saw the expanse of the entirety of the Great Earth. And as in a vision, he saw her shake herself free, as if she were spinning so fast that nothing could cling to her. And as if a white cloud poured out from the top of her and then downward and around her, forming a white ring. And he saw her spinning there.

The Fourth Vision

Then the vortex, spinning, spinning, carried him further and he saw the entire galaxy. He saw everything – the great stars, the Moon Mother and others! He saw.

He saw come flashing through this galaxy, as if lightning rods, great light! Flashing through! And he daren't wonder whence they came. He saw grandness.

The Fifth Vision

Once again the vortex spun and lifted him, and it was as if he were in another land. He saw flashes before him of this land, sparseness and sand. "Where is the great water?" he wondered.

Again and again, visions of this new land he saw. They came quickly and left. And one thought remained: "Where is the water? Where is the water?"

The Sixth Vision

And then he was lifted again, the vortex carrying him, spinning around he went. It set him once again standing atop the mountain. And again the breath! The breath within and without him. The Wind Spirit caressed his being and lifted itself away.

There presented before him a great wall of flames. He felt the beckoning and toward the flames he went and then into them. They were all around him and in him.

In the center of the flames was a pool of water into which he placed his body. And the spirit of his being remained within the flames. And there came a vision. It was as if the Earth Mother were covered with flames as she moved through the sky. There were flames coming from her. This he did see.

Then the flames faded and his body came from the pool of water once again and his spirit did reenter his body.

Once again he sang the songs, for he had seen the visions. Softly he sang the words, made the sounds.

The Seventh Vision

Soon the Moon Mother rose before him and, as in a vision, she did open wide. Golden was she inside. And then she did spin and spin, as if she would spin away. And then the vision was gone. In the place of the vision was the Moon Mother that he had seen even at his birth.

And the visions were complete.

Here he stayed until the dawning of the day, when he would carry the visions down the mountain to his people. Until then, he would be.

"Truly," he thought, "the greatness of the Great Ones has visited upon us. Truly."

CHAPTER SIX

Dear Reader

Above the stratosphere, where human form resides, above, beyond the form, there begins an entire universe. Beyond the entire universe where there is no form, there begins the unnamed. Within the unnamed there resides the essence of beings who have relinquished all forms and names of being.

Once every million years, in the time as we know it to be, the essence gathers together and descends through all forms, gathering the essential structure of each form, and then takes form upon this great Earth Mother.

The purpose of this occurrence is partly unspoken, for it is of being. The part of the purpose that can be spoken would be called "total and complete living communion."

At this occurrence, there have resulted creations of new planets, abandonment of civilizations known, engendering of new humanities. That which was before is maintained in that the essential is gathered. A new form is then presented.

The calling forth of the People from within and without the Great Mother would, if able to be completed, change the essential essence of humanity in its entirety. Therefore, the Observers assist in maintaining the light of the People and observe closely the gathering of all.

Our histories have called this change by many names. Some believe it to be but a dream. Others have claimed it to be mere fantasy. And some dare to dream the dream, hoping...hoping that the splendor of creation in its most complete form might be at hand. Some have called this "The New Beginning." Some have called this "The Garden of Eden." Some have called this "The Age of Love." Many, many want it to be. Some pray it to be. Some think it to be. Those who want and think and dream it to be are preparing for transformation. Perhaps without knowing it.

Dare you, dear reader, believe in that form of creation wherein reside total and complete love and peace of being? Can you conceive of this? Does your mind flood you with thoughts, reasonings of how it might be impossible? Turn away from those thoughts.

In the continuing occurrence, once every million years, there are increased vibrations until that which is unnamed might take form. You see the purpose for it all. You hear the purpose for it all. You know the purpose for it all.

This is the once of only once that these words have been spoken. Never before in all the forms of humanities have there been those able to hear, to know, to comprehend the depth of the occurrence.

You, dear reader, you who hear this tale, you carry this tale into your lives, perhaps unknown at first and then perhaps recognizing within yourselves the living of the tale, your living of the tale.

Those of you who hear this tale and find it in your lives are transforming even as we speak, for you are the People. For you, we have come. For you! This is your story. This is your heritage! This is the history of your being! Feel yourself remembering. Allow yourself to remember who you are. You have had those feelings since you were born! Perhaps you have thought, "Who am I, really?" "Why am I here?" "What is my purpose?"

Perhaps you have thought, "There must be a better way." Perhaps you have thought, "Will there be peace?" Yes, perhaps you have thought, "I feel trapped in this thing called my life! And a great journey beckons me. I don't know where it will take me!"

Perhaps you have thought, "Is this running away? Am I running away from this thing called reality? Where would I go? Who would I leave behind?"

Perhaps you have had these thoughts?

Then we say to you: Fear not for those you would leave behind, for we are here until the very last. There are none who would be left behind. It is your great compassion that leads you to think this way.

In the Gathering, beings of light unite. If everyone waited until the very last, where then would be the beacons of light? You see? Yes, dear ones, you are the People. This is your tale. This is your heritage. Yes!

Already in your lives, perhaps, you have changed and you don't know what you are changing toward. You only know that you are changing. Then we do speak, even to the cells of your being! This is your transformation! Yes!

Thusly we speak with you in the telling of this tale, the Story of the People. Thusly we speak with you, dear, dear ones.

CHAPTER SEVEN

The Unexpected

Location: Universal Observation Room

"Knew it! I knew it! The activity on Level Two has increased." The old man paced in front of the monitors. "Soon they'll need full support. Level Two!"

He had felt the change even before the young technician called him, and there on the screen was the blatant reason for the alarm that raced through him. Bright blue light filled the screens. There in the blue cavern, on the tables, were variating colors, illuminated beings in advanced stages of assimilation.

"There are twelve of them...twelve," he stopped his pacing for a moment. A glance at the monitors confirmed the newly increased rate. "This is going to be bigger than we planned...much bigger.

"What's the history of those forming on Level Two?" Even as he asked, the technician handed him the dossier. It too was color-coded blue. He grasped the file in one hand while his arm wiped clear a space on the table. There had never been a reason to examine this report until now.

"We will see." He scanned page after page. "We will see." His finger loudly tapped the middle of the page. "Aha! Beneath the sea! They came from beneath the sea at the beckoning long ago."

He flipped through more pages. "We'll have to see the in-depth history. How can we best support them?" he breathed into the pages. "We'll have to call another Council, to be sure, to be sure."

"The data is complete, sir."

"Call the Council." The old man looked up at the new figures. "There are those who'll already know why we're calling."

"Perhaps we should meet here, sir, then they can..."

"...see for themselves! Splendid idea! Call the Council to meet here."

As the young technician placed the call, the old man resumed his pacing in front of the monitors, pausing at each screen and thinking aloud, "It'll be very fast, their assimilation...total and complete, very fast, those twelve. Then we'll have to transport them." His experience with the unknown kept his thinking clear and concise. "We'll have to make some decisions."

The observation room quickly filled with Council members. Each one, at first sight of the glowing blue monitor screens, hurriedly stepped closer for a better look. When their leader arrived and had studied the new data, they formed a circle and began.

"And so we gather here and can see," she began. "You have demonstrated quite clearly the changes occurring." Her nod complimented the technician's work.

She turned to the old man. "Of those coming together, is there one gathering yet that can bear the presence of Level Two?"

"There is the one with our dear brother." He'd been considering the same question himself. "Soon there will be more than the three. They're very strong as they are and then there'll be the addition of those villagers. They are stout of heart. Perhaps that gathering will be able to receive those of Level Two.

"We won't know, of course," he continued, "it'll be quite timely. They'll be coming together just when Level Two will have to be preparing for transport. It will be close. That is the one possibility."

The lower row of monitors displayed the progress of various groups gathering together, and the old man's conclusions were obviously correct. She confirmed, "It appears there is none other than that. They're coming though, we can see the light building amongst them." Her heart poured out to them as she spoke to the screens, "Oh dear ones, oh."

The technician called in the observations of the golden field with the People. She spoke for them all. "The main group is powerful, maintaining quite well."

She touched her hand to the golden emblem signaling them to gather 'round. They formed a close circle as she continued, "Never could we have prepared for such an occurrence. Never would we have even jested about it. We can't really send support to the three. They're bearing as much as they're able. However, we can be present when the villagers join them; we can assist. Everything will, of course, happen quite consecutively.

"Put out those scanners," she ordered. "Even though it's doubtful, see if we can discover any other influence."

Her eyes met the gaze of each one. "Then we'll gather again at the time of the meeting with the villagers. However," she added, "at that time we must be prepared to give all the assistance we are able to give.

"Except for you of Level Three," she turned to the green representative, "you would not attend, of course. You're maintaining your own level."

The radiating colors beneath the blue glowing of the representative of Level Two demonstrated to them all the rapidity of the assimilation. "Level Two, there will be support with you, dear sister." Their leader motioned for assistance and two Council members easily lifted the glowing blue body.

She closed the meeting. "Until that time then, we depart, for there is much to do."

From the place of total darkness, these words are whispered: "Never will they know what hit them. Never will they know. This force is grand. They will never know."

As there is light, then is darkness. And in the consciousness of dissemination he resided. Well hidden, unknown, unexpected, as he always had been. The force of dissemination had also grown.

There was but one being who was aware of the possibility of the force of dissemination: the one who remembers. And even he was not aware of the increased power. Yet, he traveled with the two. Together they traveled across that mountaintop.

CHAPTER EIGHT

The Fox and the She-Wolf

Upon the light of day, the Warrior, carrying his visions with him, began the journey down the mountain to his people. As he was traveling, he came upon the encampment of the Old One, the Father of his people. His feet hadn't touched this ground for many years, but still it remained unhidden and open for him to enter.

"Dear Father of my people," he said, raising his hand in greeting, "I am here to speak with you of the visions and to bring you with me."

The Old One knew of this Warrior's coming and had already spread his blanket upon the Mother Earth. He bid him enter and sit that they might form a union together. When they were sitting across from each other, the Warrior continued. "Many visions has the Great One given to us. He beckons us to go inward, through the caverns of this great Earth Mother. And he did say to take the Old Ones with us. "Here this day, then, from the top of the mountain, I have come directly to you, saying, 'Bring only the holy blanket of your being. Leave the rest and come.' "

The Old One had known that he would be traveling. He wondered if it were time to leave this life for another. Now he heard the words and knew. "Then the time has come. The journey begins." He gathered a few roots and placed them in his satchel. "These I will bring to the encampment of our people. Then I will leave them there, for there are those who are needing these roots." He slung the strap over his shoulder. "I have been gathering them."

After the Old One had gathered his holy blanket, the Warrior blessed the place where the Old One had resided.

"Oh Great Mother, blessed are thee
That you have received this Old One.

"The blessings of your being come forward
At this place of encampment."

Without another word, they continued, the Old One and the Warrior.

Little, if at all, did they speak during the journey, for they were in communion within. When they came upon the flowing water, each stretched his arms upward in statements of praise. They took the water into their beings and then continued downward.

In their journey they came to a rise and upon the rise stood a great fox with his long tail. As they stopped to see, the fox spoke with them, saying, "Come with me." And they followed.

The fox stopped upon one spot and they saw, flowing from the Earth Mother, a liquid as they had never seen before. It was thick, as if from a flower's nectar, yet this was from an opening in the Earth Mother, an opening so large that they could place their hands within it. Nectar flowing thick, the color of blue. And they wondered at what was occurring.

The fox knew that they saw and then spoke again, "Come with me." And they followed.

Even as the fox entered the clearing, they saw. It was as if there were a hole in the Great Blue Sky, and from it was dripping golden nectar. They saw that it was thick and wondered what it could be.

Then the fox said once again, "Come with me." They followed until they came to another clearing. There appeared a hole in the Earth Mother, and flowing forth was thick, red liquid. And they wondered what it could be. Then the fox was gone, for he knew that they had seen all the three.

The Warrior and the Old One felt the immediacy to continue their journey to the People, and as they continued they spoke within their beings their thoughts to each other.

As they walked, the Great Warrior asked, "Old One, have you seen this before?"

The Old One within his being said, "Never have I seen this before."

And they continued.

In their journey downward they came to the encampment of another Old One and they entered singing.

"Old Mother of our People," said the Warrior, "Greetings with thee." They saw that she had gathered her holy blanket and was waiting.

She turned and sang the songs to the encampment that had born her, cared for her. Singing to the Earth Mother songs of love, as if a lullaby.

Even as the three walked from her encampment, the trees did bend themselves together, and where there was encampment, now were trees. Without speaking further, they continued.

Soon, great branches of a tree came across the path so that they could not pass. The Warrior said within his being, "Great Mother, have you seen this before?"

"Never," she replied.

She stepped before the great branches and sang them a song. Her soft sounds caressed the branches, and soon they parted. And there appeared before them a scene as if from another time.

They saw people gathering together, lightbeings, golden light in a great encampment. They saw the beings carrying the symbols of truth upon themselves and upon their sleeping places. They saw, too, the great light in the center of the encampment radiating the symbols. It lighted entire sky with gold. They saw.

Then the branches of the great trees closed once again. The Old One stood before them and sang the songs of praise for the gift of the vision, and they parted once again for the three to continue on their journey down the mountain.

Soon they heard below the sounds of their People, the sounds of the children. Before they could go further, there came before them a white she-wolf, white as the winter snow.

She said to them, "Come with me." She brought them to a river, and there it was as if something had torn a hole in the river. From the tear flowed thick nectar orange in color, thick nectar. They saw. Then the she-wolf was gone.

The Warrior said within his being, "Old Ones, have you seen this before?"

And they replied, "Never."

Before they entered the encampment of their People, they formed a circle in the center of a small forest. In the center of their circle came a tiny flame. There it burned while the three were sitting, each upon the holy blanket of their being.

The Warrior spoke aloud, "Oh Great One, many visions you have given us this day. Guide us."

They sat, the two Old Ones and the Warrior, in the forest and there hovered around them the spirits of the forest.

The Old One took from his satchel the three roots, and each one he placed in the flame. First the golden root, then the red root, and then the white. The essence of the roots rose upward and filled the tiny place within the forest. And the spirits of the forest flowed about in the essence.

The spirits of the forest gathered together and carried into their presence a ball of light. Soon the ball opened, first a little, like the bud of a flower. It closed and then opened a little more, like the blossom half open. It closed and then opened wide, like the blossom in full bloom. From the center of the ball, a luminescent golden blossom formed. The three saw. The spirits placed the golden blossom in the center of the flames, and the essence was carried upward.

The spirits of the forest still hovered around them while the essence of the golden blossom resided at the top of the forest in the very tips of the trees. There they rested their beings, as the time of the Moon Mother came upon them.

Dear Reader,

Know that when you hear this tale, you carry the truths within your being. Then your steps upon the great Earth Mother are golden in light. And there come those who place their feet in the golden prints whereupon you have stepped.

Dear ones, can you release attachment to all beings, trusting that none will be removed from you without your choice? Release holding them to you. They will not depart from you lest it be your choice. Even though perhaps you believe you are the caretakers of one and then another, release yourselves.

Trust these words. Relieve yourself of the grasping to them. Allow yourselves to be who you are, however you are. Know in your heart of hearts that everything and everyone is being taken care of. Everything is perfect. There is reason for everything. For every vibration. Release your attachments. Fear not for losing them. Just release, that you might be who you are. Blessings upon you.

CHAPTER NINE

Level Two of Blue

In the depths, in the bowels of the great Earth Mother, there existed a great cavern. And in the cavern resided the receiving places for twelve beings. Upon the receiving places there came together essence in life form. Essence of blue in Level Two.

They had been waiting. As they felt the flow within their beings, within their limbs, they felt the life force take form: physicality. At that moment, the knowingness of each and every being filled each form, for they were of a People who once walked upon this great Earth. Long ago, at the shaking-of-herself-free, those beings of blue had been beckoned to enter through the cavern door in the great sea. They heeded the call, entered and found the passageways beneath the sea. They traveled into the depths, the glowing of their bodies producing light enough for them to see their way. Then they came upon an opening and the first light they had seen since entering the depths. As they stood at the opening, there presented before them a new land. It was glowing and lighted as if the great sun were shining! As they stepped from the cavern and into the light, the essence of their beings tingled amongst them and they began to form a blue glowing. They looked upon their limbs and the limbs of each other and saw a thin layer of blue forming around them. When they waved their arms, it still remained around them.

The new land called them and they saw trees bearing fruit, fields, and flowing waters. Three beings like themselves came from behind the trees and greeted them with outstretched arms. Those greeting them did not speak.

The last one stepped from within the cavern and into the light. Glowing blue was she. In long strides she came to those greeting and presented herself. There was great rejoicing both within herself and within those who had come to meet them. It was as if she had come home.

She said within her mind, "What is this blue upon my being? This blue light?" Within her mind, from one of the greeters, came the answer: "It is to assist you to adjust to this atmosphere. Here it is different from the place you have come from."

She looked at her friends, wondering if they had also heard those words. They smiled with joy at her inquiring face and she knew. Then they were all thinking at once, "What place is this? Who are these beings greeting us? What is it that we would do here?"

Before the thinking could be completed, they found themselves following the beings into the valley amongst the tall grasses, the trees plentiful with fruit, and the clear waters. Soon they came upon a clearing. Twelve places there were, as if platforms in the earth.

The one who had greeted them said with his mind, "Here. Lay your bodies here. This will help you to adjust to your new home."

Some held feelings of longing for that which they had left. For some, a tiny tear trickled from their eyes. With others, joy and excitement. And with all, they laid their bodies down upon the platforms in the circle. When they did, a great blue dome formed over them. There they rested and received nourishment. There were no questions and no answers. Just being.

And here they were once again, gathering their essence in the cavern of the great Earth Mother, carrying with them a new manner of living, a new manner of being. They felt themselves take form in the cavern called Level Two.

One thought, "Filled with joy am I in this assimilation of my being. To return. Will the Earth be as it was? Will there be others?"

Another thought, "I wonder what awaits us. I had nearly forgotten this home. I had nearly forgotten."

And another, "So, now we return. And who awaits us this time?"

And so the twelve allowed themselves to assimilate, taking form in the cavern of the Earth Mother called Level Two.

Location: Climbing Toward the Light.

Soon the villagers would be at the top of the pass. They had been climbing. With much excitement, they had seen the light come closer and spill down the mountain.

The one who had begun the journey spoke. "One more day. D'ya think? One more day."

"One more day'd do it," his friend answered.

They had reached a small, flat clearing and stopped to catch their breath. This last part of the climb had been the most strenuous.

Another came up beside them. Looking upward, he studied the last part of the climb. "Then we'd be in good position to see." Sitting down on one of the smoother rocks, he added, "And yet we won't be exposing ourselves. You see there," he pointed, "there?" They were quiet for a moment. "The rest won't be so difficult, will it. Just there," he pointed again to a large pile of tumbled rocks behind which they'd be able to hide and still have a good view of the rest of the plateau.

"Then we can wait," said the first. "At night then we'll see. Tonight we'll rest here."

"Rest?" The last to reach them was still filled with the momentum of his climb. "We could continue, be there by morn!"

"No, no." The oldest member of the group spoke, "We'll rest as he says. 'Tis his plan and it's done us well 'til this time. We'll rest here. It's nearly dusk. Then we'll have our strength with us in the morn."

They spoke amongst themselves. "Look there below, into the village! See? Lights are on. They've placed lights in their windows. See?" He looked at his comrades to be sure they also saw.

"They've been watching us – and the light, no doubt! As have we!"

"Seems to've grown a bit, wouldn't you say?"

"Ya, seems to've grown brighter, too. Covers a larger area, don't ya think?"

"Could be that we're just closer."

"We are closer, though," replied the oldest one. He smiled at their friend who had planned the climb and invited them to join. "'Tis a good plan. Serves us well!"

Those villagers, stout of heart though they were, did make their final encampment on the side of the mountain. At dawn, then, they would make their final climb over the top and position themselves well so that when dusk came again, they would see the light and yet remain unseen.

Now that they were closer, they carried a bit of fear...and wonder. Yet there were those few close friends, sitting together in the encampment, who had felt different throughout the entire climb. They even remarked at it amongst each other.

"Fact was," said one, "when we came around the bend, I felt a wave of peace come over me and it's increased through the entire climb up this north face!"

They each agreed. They had each experienced the same.

The one who had made the plan from the start thought to himself, "We've come a long way. It's taken us but a few days, and here we are. One more climb."

"I wonder what it is? That light. Why is it calling me so? I dare believe that if there had been a loved one in the village below, I would have left her!" He smiled to himself. "The call is so strong. I'm thankful there was no one else to think of." He looked upward toward the top. "It just beckons me. It beckons me!"

He looked about at his compatriots. Most had already fallen into deep sleep. "Well, there they all are. We've done it together. Yet I would have come alone." He pulled a blanket over his tired body. "Are we ready? I'm ready. I speak for myself. I am ready!"

The thoughts were so loud within his mind that he looked at the others to see if they had heard and then chuckled aloud at his folly. One friend lifted his head, responding to the slight sound. Their eyes met and then in a moment he was back to sleep.

He continued his thoughts. "I want to know. What is this calling? What is this light spilling forth like nectar down the mountainside? Tomorrow I'll see."

He looked down at his village. "Those little lights below, our friends, no doubt they're wondering too." He breathed a deep sigh and settled back against the smooth rocks. "Just to go over the plan one more time, the last climb. Then I'll rest, too. One more time...."

From the darkest dark of the universe, a voice speaks:
"They will never know. They will never know. Increase. Increase. Let them feel the rumblings! They will never know."

There was only one who felt the oppressive, building force. And as the three gathered atop the mountain, it weighed heavy upon him.

"I must get to the Gathering," he thought, "I must get to the Gathering."

Even at the feeling of the increased force, he communed with the two and allowed the light to spill forth from his being, as they had been together. Once again, in the center of their tiny circle formed the symbols of light.

"Let the entire universe see," he thought. "Let them see!"

The symbols glowed brightly, pulsating, from the tiny circle, from the palms of their hands and from the centers of their foreheads. Some spun like vortexes. They radiated a great light. And yes, it spilled down the mountainside. And yes, in the village, they saw.

CHAPTER TEN

The First Battle

There was then the Gathering of the People, for they had heard the call. They came from everywhere, from the valleys, the mountaintops and the cities. First one, and then another heard the call, felt the pull within, left what he or she was doing and began the journey.

As they left, they felt a small tugging within, thoughts of family and belongings they were leaving. As they turned from looking back to looking ahead, the leaving then changed to going. And when they had traversed a little, the going changed to the journey, their journey.

When they placed their feet on their journey, deep within their beings, as if an ember had been kept burning from long ago, joy ignited and grew and filled. Soon they were filled to the brim and overflowing. They didn't know where or how far they were going. They only knew the strong feeling within — to go to the Gathering.

As they were traveling, one saw the glow of another, saw the joy pouring forth, and without a spoken word, they joined each other on the journey. Then two or three saw the glowing of each other and continued together.

From the valleys and the mountaintops they came, and at dusk twenty found themselves gathering at a clearing in the forest. It was as if they were family coming together, yet no one knew even one name. Forming a circle around the campfire, their joy of communion grew and grew until in unison they sang a chorus of sounds.

One young woman stepped into the center of the encampment and to the Earth Mother, to the Moon Mother, and to them all, she sang the Song of the Gathering. She sang of hearing the calling to begin the journey and of when they placed their feet upon the Earth Mother and traveled. She sang of meeting each other and feeling the glow and of their gathering. Each heart swelled with the sounds and the words of its own story.

A young man then stepped forward, for the music moved his limbs to dance. His body moved first this way and then that way, and he began to turn 'round and around, 'round and around. Around the campfire he moved, spinning like a vortex, dancing the Dance of the Gathering.

In hearing the sounds of song and in seeing the turning of the dance, the others felt movement within their limbs and together they began to sway. They breathed deeply their joy, their peace, their gathering and their journey together.

Before them, an Old One stepped forward into the center. There, in the light of the encampment fire, in the light of their beings, they saw his long white beard and flowing hair and felt his vibrant force.

Bending down, he opened his satchel and from it he pulled forth bread. He broke the bread into pieces and unto each he gave a piece. They ate the bread from the satchel of the Old One.

One woman walked to the center where the Old One stood, and from his satchel she removed the remaining corner of bread. She reached upward, upward, and placed within his mouth a piece of bread, and he did eat.

Then he leaned his head backward, as if he were looking upward to the great sky and stars above, and he began to laugh. Deep laughter filled his whole being, and those around him, and the entire encampment.

They began to embrace each other. First one and then another met the eyes of someone across the great circle. In a moving rhythm, they walked toward each other and embraced and laughed together. As they moved, little did they know that they walked the symbols upon the Earth. They simply walked in joy, embracing each other and releasing laughter.

As the evening became deep night, they settled themselves in a circle once again, lying down for rest around the campfire. Each being was fulfilled. Each one was filled with joy at the meeting of the others. They rested. When they were asleep, those symbols they had walked radiated great light in the night.

Not any knew of the growing power of dissemination. There were those who felt a growing force separate from their own, yet each was so involved with the immediacy of the occurrences within their own lives. Little did they know of the growing power of the force of dissemination.

The dark globe approached. It came upon the encampment of those who had just celebrated with joy. Without a breath of a sound, it lowered down and settled into the center of the flames. There it remained and soon the flames were no more.

Then, like the dark petals of the blackest flower, the globe opened wide, unfurling its petals. Flowing from the center rolled black essence. It filled the entire encampment, flowing around where they had danced and sung, flowing around where they had laughed together and embraced each other. It covered them all. Then outward it went, into the trees of the forest, then upward and outward. Gently, softly the blackness moved.

A man awakened and said, "The fire's out." As he raised himself to stir the embers, he looked around and saw others moving and looking at each other. He thought, "Someone let the fire go out!"

As he walked toward where the campfire was, he felt himself wonder, "What am I doing here anyway? Who are all these people? I don't even know them. I don't even know one name," he thought. Before he could actually stir one tiny remaining ember, he threw down the stick and off he went, away from those he didn't know, into the forest, wandering and wandering.

Not one called to him. Not one went after him. They all were gathering their things together and looking about to see that no one saw what they had, what they were placing in their satchels.

One young woman thought, "I must be on my way." Without turning back, she began to walk away into the forest. Then another and another, not even looking each other in the eyes. "Who are these beings?" they each thought. "What am I doing here? I have things to do." They all departed...except for one.

"I believe I'm lost." He was a young boy, the youngest of them all. "I don't even know where the forest is. Everyone else seems to know where they're going. I feel lost. I wonder if I could find my home," he said aloud to the empty encampment.

Then he saw in the center one tiny ember. He thought, "If I could have just a little light...." He crawled under the darkness and with a small stick, he poked the ember just a little. He crouched down, bending closely, and placed his face near the ember. Slowly and softly, he breathed his breath upon the ember.

It glowed. Even though all around there was deep darkness, it glowed. The boy broke his little stick and placed the pieces upon the ember and blew his breath again. A tiny fire began, with little flames flickering. He broke another piece and another piece and placed them atop the flames.

It was as if he were under a blanket of darkness. It was heavy and thick. In the dim light, he saw another stick beside him and a few small pieces. He collected them and placed them on the little flames, and they grew and grew. The darkness lifted a little. The thickness, the heaviness lifted a little.

The great dark essence of the black blossom began gathering itself together and returning to the center. From the tops of the trees, from the forest, from around the encampment it came. When it had all flowed back to the center, the great blossom closed, pulling its petals up around itself. Then without a slight hint of a sound, it lifted upward, upward, upward. The thick heaviness rose with it.

There in the encampment was one, the young boy, feeding the fire. A little stick here and there, and it grew and grew, lighting the encampment. He felt a little better inside and breathed a deep breath, still sitting close to the fire.

There were no other sticks around him, and he reached outward to find some. "Perhaps a little larger," he thought. "If I could just find a little larger...." As he reached outward, his hand felt something. He grasped it and brought it into the light. "A piece of bread," he thought.

As he lifted the bread and looked at it more closely, a feeling moved within him. He began to remember a little. He smelled the bread and it filled him.

He placed it in his mouth and it fed his being. As the nourishment flowed through him, he began to remember something. It was as if it were so distant, so distant. And yet, he was remembering something.

He placed another stick on his fire, and as the flames grew, he looked around. He saw where there had been a great circle around the campfire. As if from a far distance came a memory. It began to fill his being. He remembered that there had been others around. He turned around and looked. In his memories, he saw them sitting around him. Then they faded.

He remembered the dancer, dancing around. A little flicker, here and there. "Could there have been a dancer? Here where I am standing?" He turned around. He took a larger stick and placed it in the flames until it was a torch. Holding it high above his head, he walked around the encampment.

"Yes! I do remember! Yes! And the singer! I remember the sounds, the song, the song!" Slowly the words returned to him, the words of the song, of the journey, of the leaving, of the going, of the coming. He remembered. He remembered the Old One, standing in the center, and his great laughter. He smiled a little at the memory. When he smiled, a tiny fluttering happened within his being. It was something...something...it began to fill him. Soon he felt that he was all right. "Oh, yes, I remember now," he said. "I am placing my feet upon this journey!"

Soon he was filled to the brim and overflowing. He felt it and he emanated light. It was a tiny light, yet he was glowing once again. He ran around the encampment calling, "Hello! Are you there? Is anyone there? Don't you remember? Where are you all? Don't you remember?"

Around and around he ran, holding the lighted stick above his head. He saw no one. He heard no one. He was the only one. Where they had all gone, he didn't know. He was the only one.

There, in the center of the encampment, was the satchel of the Old One. He looked at it for a time and then walked to it. It wasn't so much that he wondered what was inside, it was that he just wanted to touch it, to feel it. Yet, as he reached it, he placed his hand inside. He felt something.

"What's this?" He felt something round, like a disc. He felt his hand grasp onto it. It fit right into his hand. He removed it from the satchel and leaned forward toward the campfire to examine it. It was a disc that fit right into his hand.

It felt a little heavy and yet a little light. He examined it closely. There seemed to be something on it, some kind of scratchings. "Perhaps it's the name of the Old One," he thought. He turned it to look at the other side, and there in the center was a symbol. Even while he held the disc, the symbol began to radiate light. It seemed to come alive for him.

Light poured forth, first a little and then a little more. Symbols of light began to form. They radiated, reflecting onto the face of the young boy. He grasped the disc in his hand and held it to him. Yes. Yes.

He took the woven piece of material attached to the disc and placed it over his head. The disc fell upon him exactly upon his heart. As it radiated, he felt the strength of the symbols flow through him.

Beside the satchel was the staff of the Old One. He saw it. Closing the satchel, he placed the staff atop it and breathed a deep breath. He turned away from the satchel, the staff, and the fire. "I must continue this journey," he thought.

Just as he was about to leave the encampment, he turned to look once again. That staff beckoned him. He returned and lifted it. It felt strong in his hand. It felt very strong in his hand. He lifted it upward for a moment and then placed one end on the ground beside his foot, the other end upward toward the sky. It felt right. In his mind he heard the words, "This unto you I bestow."

He felt the staff, he felt the disc upon him, and in his mind he remembered once again the Old One leaning his head backward and laughing a great laugh. He thought three times in his mind, "Thank you, Old One."

The boy continued on his journey. He didn't know exactly where he was going, yet he did know something. "I'm going now," he thought, "and whereever I am going, I will certainly arrive. And certainly there will be others!"

As he placed his feet upon the Earth Mother, a light formed, and if one were to look, one would see where he had walked. Yet, there was no one to see. Not one saw the golden steps he placed upon the Earth Mother.

As he walked, he sang the song of his journey, as had the young woman who had sung the song of the journey to the Gathering. Once and then twice, he leaned his head backward and allowed deep laughter to come. And when it did, he grasped the staff tightly and remembered nearly everything. In him, there was not even a wondering of the darkness that had settled over them, over him. He did remember though, nearly everything. He grasped firmly to the staff.

He continued onward as did many, many. The journey of light, toward the light. He felt it calling him. Others felt the call. Yes, they continued – one here, the number of a hand there, the number of three hands there. This one young boy, one from twenty, carried the essence of that encampment. He ventured onward. Blessed be the ones who venture onward.

There was one who remembered everything. He felt the occurrence even without being there, and he knew what had happened at the encampment. "I must get to the Gathering," he thought. The other two with him felt the urgency, not knowing why. Yet they felt the urgency.

As the three sat together, he spoke aloud to them. "Soon," he said, "there will be others coming. Soon they will be here. Perhaps at dawn, perhaps at dusk, they'll be meeting us. This I do know." The other two felt that he was speaking the truth. They radiated light together, the three. Yet he said nothing of the rest....

In the village below, those watching the moving light whispered amongst themselves, "It's almost at the North Pass. The light is almost there!" Some looked with wonder. One woman wrung her hands. A child pointed and whispered, "My father is there." They all wondered and remembered those six of their village who had departed but a few days before.

Still, even in their wondering, the light spilled forth down the mountain and into the village, nearly onto the little streets of stone, nearly onto the carts.

CHAPTER ELEVEN

The Great One Returns

In the great golden field, surrounded by trees erect as themselves, were the People, emanating and vibrating the symbol they had taken to themselves lest they forget who they are.

His call resonated throughout the field and into the trees and to where the river was flowing. They heard and joyfully turned from what they were doing. Some had been caressing those rocks upon the riverbank, singing sweetly and softly to them. A few had been studying markings of other life forms to gain great knowing of the beings who made them. And others assisted in maintaining the large blue cocoons.

They knew He would return as He had promised. Their hearts filled with thoughts of their Great One. They gathered at the rise in the field, each one resonating the truth of the symbol he or she carried upon himself.

Some sat upon the large rocks, others remained standing as they waited. Even before they saw Him, they felt the essence of the One within themselves. They called Him "the One," simply because there was no name. And yet, that of no name gathered essence in form. Before them, as if a star gathering its rays into itself, their Great One appeared in physical form.

His great light showered upon them. "I come to prepare the way, I come to prepare the way, you are as children. Hear these words." His deep voice filled them and awakened their sleeping minds.

"You place these markings upon your beings. You vibrate those markings and the truths therein lest you forget who you are." He moved closer to them. "And in so doing, even a part of you forgets!"

It was not what they had expected. They daren't look to one another with questioning eyes. As if in a winter shower, they felt the intensity of His presence as He walked among them.

"Know you not the darkness is upon you? Even a tiny trickle forms within you!" They shrank away from His words.

"You placed your feet upon this great Earth Mother and deigned that light essence take form," He motioned to their glowing bodies, "yes, in your physical form." Their innocence begged to understand. "You gathered together and walked the truths because you *are* the truths. That is the purpose."

"Yes," they thought, "that is what we do." All remembered the day when they had first stated the purposes. How could they be forgetting? And what of the darkness?

"Hear these words: *When you walk the truths lest you forget them, then you have forgotten.* You see? Dear ones, it is the nature of physicality."

He raged amongst them, His voice bellowing, waving His arms with each statement. "Cast aside the rules you have created so that you would not forget!" He pointed to the markings in the Earth. "Cast aside those drawings you have made so that you would not forget the symbols of truth!"

He grabbed one to Him and rubbed the marking from his chest and another and wiped the colored marking from her face. "Remove these drawings from your beings!"

In just a few steps He was at the cocoons. "Remove these symbols from the resting places!" Even as He spoke, the forms began to fade.

He outstretched His arms and a light greater than the sun surrounded him. "Hear these words:

> YOU ARE THE TRUTH!
> YOU ARE THE TRUTH.
> YOU ARE THE TRUTH.

"When you depend on these slight things to remember, then you have given up remembering! Given up being! You see, dear ones?"

They felt His words enter their beings. Bursts of light filled them as He continued.

> "YOU ARE WHO YOU ARE.
> YOU ARE WHO YOU ARE.
> YOU ARE THE TRUTH."

Then there was silence. They felt the words echoing within themselves and through the field and trees and flowing waters. He gently gathered them around Him and sat with them.

"You resonate and walk upon this great Earth Mother." His soft voice caressed them. "When you walk, you do form the symbols. You know this to be true. However, when you first came here, there was not the consciousness that you would be practicing forms and symbols. You walked in the newness of your being from the very caverns. Didn't you come? You walked together, being the truth. Each one. Being.

"And then, dear ones, didn't you divide yourselves? Each one a symbol? And in doing so, you created emptiness. For when you turn away from the others and you face but one truth and you vibrate that one truth, then you have beckoned darkness within your being. You see? For darkness is separation. It is little more. It is the nature of darkness. It is the purpose of darkness. Know you this? No, you name it not.

"You say that perhaps you would forget like the others. Such innocence! It is the nature of physicality! And yet, we deign to bring form so that there might be totality on this great Earth Mother. Totality! In totality, then know you this: neither darkness nor light resides. There is total and complete union. Total and complete union. There are no sides, remembering and forgetting. There is one.

"We say to you, prepare yourselves. Remove that symbol of separation from your being! And be."

They began to understand, and even as He spoke there were those who rubbed the symbols from their beings. Others wondered and He heard their wonderings and replied, "Yes, even that thought of 'What if we do not walk the truths as we have been?' enters. You have been on this Earth Mother barely full time and yet you wonder." As if to Himself He repeated, "Tis the nature of physicality.

"Here we do say: Then comes unity. Then comes beyond unity: One. Simply continue to be, dear ones. If you were to walk anew, then the symbol that you walk would be the symbol of truth *because you have walked it.* You see? You see who you really are?

"If you were to walk anew, and patterns of light take form and resonate then those new patterns would be the truths. Whatever you walk would be the truths! For you are who you are...you *are* the truths. You see? You see?"

They sat together in silence for a very long time and just when they were about to stir, He rose and moved to the spot where He had first taken form.

"Soon there will be others. You, lightbeings, are the People, and yet soon there will be others. They are coming because they simply must. They have been heeding the call and they must come."

A whirling sound came around Him and He spoke the words from within the vortex.

"Then we say unto you, that which appears to be battle would be union. You know not these words, for you know not even battle itself, dear ones. Yet at that moment you would hear these words again within your being resonating, perhaps then you would know.

"Wonderful are you, vibrating truths."

Even though His form was no longer with them, His essence filled them and filled them to overflowing, so great was His light.

Location: Council Meeting

She touched the emblem on her robe and began. "We have called this Council once again so that we would speak of the most recent occurrences."

They had gathered in the Council room and their leader met the gaze of each as she spoke. "We speak only now of the building of force. Each one has felt the presence and we have initiated the next phase.

"Even as we speak, there is one of us taking form and giving guidance to the gathering of the People." She waited until their whisperings ceased. It was early to be directly assisting the People, and yet.... "Our procedures have come sooner than we had planned. What appeared to be a plan followed by observation has changed." She tossed the project papers aside. "There is, or appears to be, something else occurring, something that has greatly affected the turning, that has greatly affected assimilation."

She hadn't been prepared for these changes, and even though her outward appearance was according to their custom, her thoughts and feelings were a little disheveled. She spoke her wonderings aloud. "Perhaps we of the Council are also being observed and yet we don't know it. There are those who have carried this theory in their hearts; now we speak of it. Something else is also occurring, and it appears we are observers." She cleared her thoughts and then said, "Let us speak of the observations."

Her old friend from the observation room could barely contain himself. "We have each had our own theories, dear sister. Yet, one day a change occurs and we believe that a theory has been proven or disprove. I wave away those theories, each and everyone! Let us speak of observations!"

All eyes focused on the old one as he continued, "Yes, yes, let's speak of observations. Level Two is nearly assimilated. Who will receive them? Our dear friend is gathering together, emanating the light. He is strong, for the remembrance brings strength.

"Yes, as we have spoken, they are gathering together — Level Two and our brother, simultaneously, it seems. They'll be gathering together and receiving Level Two all in one breath.

"And if that news were not enough to raise our concern, even as we speak, as our dear sister has informed us, another dear brother is presenting guidance to the People. Such innocence of being they are!

"And then, of course, it appears the only level that can be on schedule—" a twinkle escaped his eyes, "we jest of course — Level Four is dormant." Chuckling aloud, he continued, "You see, some things are the same." He knew his humor offered little relief from the intensity of the meeting.

"Level Three," he went on, turning toward those representatives of green, "we have been observing your work in maintaining activity. Good work. It appears it might maintain itself."

As he stood, they felt his strength. "What we have been observing is as we expected...truly." He looked around at their questioning faces. "What is this concern? It is occurring. Simply, it is occurring."

His words roused their spirits. "Remember the celebration! The time is at hand! It is now! We want so desperately that this gathering be the one, that we have forgotten the celebration, that it is the time of the Gathering!"

He spoke slowly and deliberately, "We could listen to our own guidance to the People, for even as I speak with you, this Council, dear brothers and sisters, the words that are spoken with the People would be spoken here, lest we forget: *This is the Gathering!*"

He paused for a moment. "It is, in and of itself, the Gathering. Dare we think it would take the same form as every other? Rejoice! It is different! Rejoice! Perhaps this is the one!"

Their thoughts joined him as he returned to his seat, yet he paused only for a moment before turning the attention back to the Council's leader. "What of the others, what of the others?"

She breathed deeply. "The Gathering is taking form. Those lightbeings are hearing the call and are coming forth." She spoke of the first battle, saying, "Once there was darkness where there was light, and yet that light did return. This we have observed." A smile transformed her face. "Yes, we could simply say it is the time of the Gathering of the People."

Even as the Council spoke together, each considering the reports of the others, they felt within themselves a growing force, growing vibrations, of the strength within. Yet it was so subtle they hardly knew to speak of it. Growing strength.

And the People? They cast aside the symbols and markings they had preserved, and as they did, that which had begun to be known as fear was replaced by joy. As each one cast aside the need to remember, then they did remember. They raised their arms of light and together danced in the joy of their beings and they did unite and vibrate together once again.

They lifted their voices in sound. In their great circle, they sang the Song of Union and they sang the Song of Knowing. As their sounds resonated, the light of their beings grew and grew: one light.

At the time of the Moon Mother, they formed in the center one large cocoon of light. They rested together, golden light emanating one light, one truth, one being. As they rested, essence formed within the cocoon and they then knew the truth: much more than the People were they.

In this manner they prepared.

And you, readers of this story, know that this is your story. You believe you know who you are in the story. You see? You believe you know who you are. And yet, you have heard the call. When there is releasing of fears, there is more than remembering. Then there is knowing. It is the nature of physicality.

Blessed be those who hear the call and come, believing that they know who they are. Blessed be those beings.

CHAPTER TWELVE

The Warrior Gathers His People

At the dawning of the light, the Great Warrior and the Old Ones rose and within their encampment they sang the Song of Praise to the encampment for receiving and cradling their beings. As they continued their journey, neither did they eat nor drink, for it was a short distance to their people. As they entered into the village, there were those who saw the Great Warrior and hailed him with much joy and reverence.

Then there came the two Old Ones. His people gathered around them all, for they knew, simply by seeing the Old Ones.

Their Great Warrior spoke:

"Oh my people,
The Great One has given us stories,
The Great One has given us visions.

"Upon the Great Mountain I did stand,
And then appeared to me the Great One.
Visions he did give me,
A gift to you, my people.

"Of the visions, we will speak.
Yet now we say
The Old One has said
It is time to be moving encampment."

As he spoke, the Old One viewed her people. She felt the ripple of knowingness through them. She returned her gaze to the Warrior.

"The Great One has said that we would gather, and with our dear Old Ones we would enter the cavern and go inward into this great Earth Mother; that we are to bring with us but our sleeping blanket. Nothing else.

"Our people, hear these words: We must do this. Even as we speak, we delay."

He spoke of the urgency with which the Great One had spoken to him. He told of the words the Great One had spoken.

And then the Old One, the Father of the People, stepped forward and said to them that he had not seen them with his eyes for many risings of the Moon, and yet he knew them well. He said that they would make an encampment even as he spoke. And they formed a circle. He said to the Great Warrior, "Here then, we will speak of the visions."

The Great Warrior began to tell his tale of the visions of the Mother Earth and of all the pictures the Great One had given him, had given to the People.

He sang his song in praise of the visions, in praise of his people's receiving the visions, for he knew the Old One and the wisdom of the Old One. Even though he would have gathered his people and gone to the entrance and there spoken of the visions, he knew the Old One and the wisdom, and he did speak.

And when he had finished his song of praise for his people's receiving the visions, then the Old One stepped forward once again and spoke of the visitation of the Great Fox and the visions therein. The Old One danced the Dance of Praise, the People receiving the visions.

Then the Mother of the People spoke of the She-Wolf and the vision. With her hands she clapped together the sounds and rhythms in praise of her people's receiving the words from her being.

When all the visions had been spoken, then the People raised themselves in praise of themselves. The Great Warrior spoke, saying, "Oh Great One, these are your people." Then each of them knew without a moment's hesitation that they would gather their blankets together and be on the journey. Leaving everything else, they began together.

As the last being stepped from their encampment, they turned and sang the Song of Praise of the Encampment which had borne them and cared for them, that the Mother Earth would allow them to be.

Turning, they continued. They were the People following the Great One. The Great Warrior and the two Old Ones leading the way, they began the journey upward.

One young man had known a cavern, and he thought perhaps that cavern which he knew was the opening toward which they traversed. And yet, he said nothing.

Coming upon flowing waters, they each went to the edge and, cupping their hands, placed the waters upon their being, within and without.

Within three days, they arrived at the opening.

The Great Warrior turned to his people. "This, then, is where the great Earth Mother parts herself that we might enter. Here, oh People, here we enter."

In the light of day they saw the opening in the red rocks, barely hidden by a few slender trees. The Wind Spirit moved through the tiny leaves and they flickered and clicked together. They saw the shadow of the entryway to the unknown. Yet it was without fear that they came upon this journey, for they knew

the holiness of the Earth Mother and the blessings of the Great One. Their
Warrior spoke again:

"Oh Great People," he said,
"Breathe the great blue sky,
Breathe it into your being,
That you might know.

"Oh Great People," he said,
"Breathe in the trees as you see them below,
Breathe them into your being.

"Oh Great People," he said,
"Gather this great Earth Mother in your hands,
And feel her in the light of day,
Feel her as the Wind Spirit blows upon her.

"Oh Great People," he said,
"Feel yourselves as you are,
Feel yourselves standing,
Placing your feet upon this great Earth Mother.
For this day,
We turn toward standing anew,
Breathing anew;
For this journey begins here,
Where the great Earth Mother has parted her being
That we might enter.

"Sit ye on these words."

He had felt within his people the longings. And they did, each one, feel and
breathe.

Then the Old One, the Mother of the People, spoke, gathering them about
her, touching one cheek, caressing one head, holding one hand, smiling at one
child. Round about she did go amongst them and they felt her love flowing and
they met her gentle gaze.

Almost as if in a whisper she said to them, "Has not this great Earth Mother
cared for us? And now she invites us inward. What a blessing we have amongst
us."

And then she began, as they gathered around her, to speak the story. "When
I was a child," she said, "my mother did take me about the encampment, that
I might know all the People of the encampment.

"Yes," she said, "I knew all of their fathers and all of their Old Ones. That is why I can speak to you, my children, for you are the children of the children of the children."

She spoke of the different fathers and mothers of each being, reminding them of the fathers of their fathers, reminding them of the mothers of their mothers, speaking of the traditions, the gathering of the herbs, the gathering of the roots, speaking of the traditions of weaving the blanket of sleeping. Speaking of the traditions of the children, the teaching of the children, the teaching of the children of the singing of the Song of Praise.

This she spoke with them, and they felt the love of the mother of the mother of the mother of the mother flowing, for she was indeed the Old One.

And when she had completed telling her story and the traditions and the teachings of the children, then once again she embraced them, a look here, a caressing of the cheek here, holding this hand.

She gathered in her arms one child and breathed the breath into the child. She sang the Song of Praise to the child, for this child was the newest being of the Gathering. And then, with the child in her arms, she spoke again to her people.

"This one will walk in the light of day.

This one will carry the traditions.

This one will teach the teachings.

This one will sing the Song of Praise.

See that you teach this one *everything*."

Into the arms of her people she placed the child and they all sang the Song of Praise to the little one. When they had finished, she returned to where the Great Warrior was standing. She kissed his brow, pulling him to her. "Son of the sons of the sons, you are of mine," she said.

He viewed his people. He saw the Mother of his people and he saw that they were whole and they were one.

Then the Old One, the Father of his people, stepped forward. He began the dance, the dance of his father's father of the father's father. He danced the dance upon the Earth Mother.

And when he had finished, he began to speak the story of the journey. He spoke of the father's fathers who came upon this great land, bringing his people. He spoke of how they traveled across the mountains and how they saw the encampment of the People.

He said that he had been but a child and he spoke of how they each carried him and spoke of the teachings with him, the teachings of the journey. "For on the journey there was," he said, "upon the rising, the singing of the Song of Praise of Awakening. On the journey, there was the teaching of the placing of the feet upon the Earth Mother. On the journey there was the teaching of dancing the dance upon the great Earth Mother. The time was the end of light, the beginning of Moon Mother."

He spoke with them of the teachings of the journey and as he spoke he drew pictures and symbols, and they did see. And when he had completed the telling of the story of the journey, he spoke of the journey of the father of the fathers of his people until he came, in his story, to the place of their encampment.

He walked amongst them and gathered in his arms a child. He placed the child's feet upon his own and, holding the child to him, began slowly to dance the Dance of the People, his people. Soon he and the child were one in the same space, same dance, same breath. The People knew and saw the teaching. He danced the symbols, and when they were completed he sang the Song of Praise for his people.

Holding the hand of the child, he brought him to stand where the Great Warrior stood. "Son of the son of the sons, you are of mine," he said to the Great Warrior.

The Great Warrior saw that he would let his people be. They prepared for rest, for in the rising of the light in the morn they would enter. Then they would enter, for the Earth Mother opened herself to them and beckoned that they enter. Even as he thought of the Old Ones and his people, he knew this to be the greatest journey. And yes, he also rested, placing his being upon the Great Earth, allowing her to comfort him, to fill him with peace. And so he was.

Then we would say to you, dear reader, ask yourselves — who are the others? Where are the others? Ask of yourselves to lift up your heads and hearts that you might see each other, traversing, that you might gather together, even in the daily rhythm of your lively vibration. Go you into your day and know within your heart of hearts that you are the People. Remember who you are.

Lament not for that which you have forgotten. Sing the Song of Praise for that which you have remembered, that you might breathe upon that tiny ember and it might grow and grow and fill your being. And sing the Song of Praise to the tiny ember and the blowing thereupon.

Sing the Song of Praise for the light within your being. Sing the Song of Praise for the great Earth Mother upon which you reside. Sing the Song of Praise for your own self, to your own self, for who you are.

Sing the Song of Praise for the questions unanswered and let them be, for it is believed that whereupon we find the answers, then we remember. Sing the Song of Praise for unanswered questions, for therein lies remembrance. The answers to your questions will not provide memories. Answers provide more questions, provide more answers, provide more questions....

Know you who you are and sing the Song of Praise for the remembrance. Know you who you are. Hear the story. Feel the story. It is your story, your heritage, your people, you.

Not in fear, prepare yourself; in great joy and the singing of praise then be, for the great Earth Mother shakes herself free. Sing the Song of Praise of being and be. Be.

CHAPTER THIRTEEN

The Coming and the Going

Hear ye, those who hear this tale, hear ye these words: The time is at hand. The Gathering approaches. Know you, you are the People. You are the People, and you have been gathering.

'Twas nearly dawn when the one who had created the plan for the North Pass began. He thought about every move he would make, he thought of the others and of their strength. He thought, "We've done fairly well and I still feel strong."

Even as he thought the words, he felt a strength grow within him. He felt a kind of excitement, and yet peace. There was a tiny flicker; through his mind it went: "I could be on this climb for many more days and be filled with peace."

As he felt the flicker go through his mind, he looked below to the village. The lights were on, the People were stirring. His friends, his friends were awakening also, as he. Atop this mountain he felt within his being...freedom.

He looked a moment longer and then turned his thoughts to the climb. The others with him prepared themselves also, for each had awakened just before the rising of the light and they, too, thought of the climb. Yet nary a one dared to think beyond reaching the top, nary a one.

Oh, they hadn't forgotten their purpose, yet nary a one spoke of it. They gathered their things and began. Just as they placed their feet on the journey upward, they turned to each other. Still nary a word did they speak. They looked long, long looks into each other's eyes. Then they stepped upward.

The continued upward and upward. The North Pass was a good plan. Each was, even then, surprised at his abilities to climb. One remembered the words of his friend who had said, "I am not a goat!" That friend remained in the valley and here he was, climbing. "Perhaps I am a goat," he thought in his mind and laughed a little to himself. "Perhaps I am."

Then, reaching his hand downward to assist his friend, each helping the other, they continued the climb. They stopped twice on the way upward, on the face of the North Pass to rest, to eat nourishment, and it was nearly the rising of the Moon Mother when they came over the top.

Not even a breath of relief did they breathe when the last of them was there, but positioned themselves about. One behind a rock here, two together there. They waited, waited to see for themselves.

They heard sounds coming. "What was that?" They stretched themselves and still could not see the young boy climbing over the top. They couldn't yet hear the soft sound he was making to himself.

The young boy stood, looking outward and then down at the village below. "Could this be the end of this journey?" he asked himself aloud. He placed the end of his staff beside his foot and began. He began the song, first softly, singing the song of his journey, of his leaving, of his traveling and of the Gathering. When his being was filled with joy at the remembrance of the Gathering, his voice soared. He sang the words of the Gathering, of their joy, of their light. The sounds flowed from him and filled the top of the mountain. They even spilled forth into the village below.

Those climbers behind the rocks heard. "What was that song?" they whispered to each other and moved a little closer so that they might see who was singing that song.

When the boy had sung the words of his journey, even unto the climbing to the top of this mountain, he placed his hand on the vibrating disc and, leaning back his head, he laughed a deep laugh.

The men behind the rocks chuckled a little amongst themselves at the laughter coming from the boy. The boy heard their rustling and turned toward the rocks. He called out in his innocence. "Hello," he said. "Hello. Who is there?"

From behind the rocks they came, first one and then another, until all six were standing together in the clearing. They saw the glowing emanating from the young boy and wondered if perhaps it was the setting of the sun which caused the glow. Yet the entire clearing was lighted. They moved closer to see.

As he saw them stepping forward, the boy felt the disc within his hand vibrating. The voice came within his mind, the voice of the Old One: "Show them."

He turned his hand outward so that the disc was facing the others. The glowing light burst forth into the clearing and onto their faces. A little spilled into the village.

They wondered, "Could this be the light that we came to see? It's so small." They thought, "This couldn't be it. Yet, what is that light? And who is this boy?"

Location: The Three

At the rising of the Moon Mother, the three traversing together continued their journey, for the one who remembered everything felt the villagers and the boy gathering. To the two others he said, "Best we continue. They're gathering even as we be." Even before he said the words, the two knew they would continue. They barely paused a moment.

Even though it was in the rhythm of their journey to gather together and commune in the light, sharing the symbols, the light ever-increasing, and then lay themselves down to rest at the rising of the Moon Mother, this night they continued. Slowly they stepped, one after the other, upward, upward toward the top.

Location: Observation Room

"Ah! More unexpected events!"
"And who is that?"
"Who is that boy with the light?"
"We won't call the Council yet. Not quite yet. Let's see a little more first."

Location: The Warrior and His People

At the opening of the Earth Mother resided the Old One, Mother of her people, and the Old One, Father of his people, until once again the dawn of the light came upon them.

In the slight light of the Moon Mother, their people breathed the truth of their being, the truth of their story, the truth of their heritage, the truth of their Old Ones and the truth of their Great Warrior.

Location: Leader of the Council, Speaking to the Council

"It is good that Level Three of green is not activating quickly."
"There are many unexpected events."
"For now, we can only observe."

Location: The Gathering of Lightbeings, the People.

The People on this day walked together in the joy and freedom of themselves, and as they walked they formed a new symbol, their own symbol, for they were the People.

This night they turned toward the great blue cocoons and entered there for resting. Together, two in this one and three in this one, they entered and rested.

Once again, in the center of the encampment, the lighted form radiated – a new form, a new symbol, as if a staff formed, standing on end, and then across the top lay another. The staff across the top began to spin around and lines of blue light sprayed from each of the ends. Spinning and spinning, flowing from the ends, until the lines were one, one light, one symbol, of the People.

CHAPTER FOURTEEN

And They Gathered Together

Even in the darkness, under the light of the bare slip of the Moon Mother, the three continued. The one who remembered led the way and the two, the teacher and the boy, placed their feet in his lighted steps.

Even though the two felt his urgency, they traveled closer to each other than to him. As they neared the top, they saw a small glow of light. It appeared that they had come upon a gathering!

The sounds of their approach beckoned the attention of the others who were there, and they each turned to see what was causing the sounds. They saw the three entering into the encampment. The villagers, still glowing with the reflection of the light from the young man's disc, wondered.

The first, the one who had made the plan from the start, stepped forward one step, a little hesitantly, and then another step and another. And even though in his thinking he couldn't reason why he was so attracted to the three, he felt it within his being. He felt it deeply.

Soon he was standing in front of them and with no introduction he said aloud, "You are they, aren't you? You, you are the ones, aren't you?" Even though he looked questionly from one to the other, he knew within his heart that they were indeed the ones he had traveled here to see.

The one who remembered everything stepped forward and spoke to the villager. "Yes. Yes, we are." They gazed deeply into each other's eyes.

A ripple went through the other five villagers. The Old One, the teacher, walked toward them. It was as if he had known them for a very long time, the way he approached with one arm upward and outward.

They stood and watched, wondering who this was and also wondering, "What were those words of their compatriot? What did he mean, 'You are the one?' What is this?" they thought.

When the Old One, the teacher, came closer, he spoke even as he moved about them. "Well, you've had a long climb, haven't you? Come along here." Even as he walked amongst them, he belayed their fears. "Come along, out here." It was as if their own father walked amongst them. "Yes, yes. It is good to be with you." He placed his hand on one shoulder, grabbed another hand and squeezed and released, placed his hand atop the head of another, clapped lightly the back of another. Yes, he moved amongst them. Even though in their thinking they couldn't figure out who this one was, in their heart of hearts they did feel.

And one chuckled even to himself, "This old goat has loving feelings for this man." When the teacher turned toward him, they gazed a moment at each other and then embraced! They laughed out loud together as they embraced. The others smiled, feeling the warmth. Standing in the center, the young man with the staff leaned his head backward and laughed a deep laugh from within his being.

The young boy of the three came to the one with the staff, for he had heard the singing of the Song of the Journey and he had felt within himself the soaring of the words and the sounds of the Gathering, and he came to him.

It was as if he were looking at his own self. As he stood directly across from that one he thought, "The one of the song – so he is the one of the song." And yet, as he met his gaze directly, he knew he was much more.

The disc on the young boy vibrated and a light came once again, so strongly, it nearly lighted the entire gathering. The boy standing directly across felt the glow. He placed his hands upward, opened, toward the disc. From his hands came beams of light, and the light grew and grew.

The one who remembered, with his arm around the shoulder of the villager, turned toward the two young ones in the center. The villager saw and he knew that the light for which he had come was here. As he thought, he felt the arm move from his shoulder and he looked. He looked at the one who remembered everything and he saw in the center of his forehead a beam of light. It radiated across to the Old One, to that Old One with his compatriots. The Old One stood, and the light between the two grew and grew.

Soon he felt the urge. He felt it as strongly as he had felt the urge to come on this climb up the North Pass and to the top and to here, to this Gathering. He stepped forward and stood in the center and the light, the light between the Old One and the one who remembered everything spilled upon him, and the light between the young one and the one with the disc spilled upon him, for he was in the center. Beams of light radiated upon him and he felt the glow. He felt something within his being growing and growing and growing. It was something like the joy he felt, and yet it was more. He was being filled! He was being filled with light!

Soon he radiated the light as a beacon from every part of his being. Then he stepped toward his compatriots. At first they shrunk away a little, but then one stepped forward. It was as if the ember within him had received a slight blowing from the Wind Spirit. He felt it and he stepped forward toward his friend. As he did, he stepped between the beams of light and he, too, felt the flowing.

And then another and another stepped forward until each one in turn stood in the center. Even unto the last, himself thinking, "This old goat, this old goat am I." And he stood in the beams of light and he, too, was filled.

They formed a circle together and the one who remembered everything radiated. From the center of his heart formed the symbols, and even as he began, all of the others began. In the heart of every being the symbols formed and radiated into the center.

The symbols changed and changed, each one appearing. As the light grew, the symbols formed themselves, light symbols standing on end. Great symbols, growing larger and larger, so that even those in the circle looked upward to view the entire symbol...of truth.

The great light spilled forth and down the mountain. Just as one compatriot thought, "The villagers will see this light. They'll be viewing this light, as we did in the beginning. They'll be wondering about this light...and here I am. Here we are! Radiating light!"

Before he could speak, before he could think even another thought, there came from above..."What was that above?" he thought. "What was that above?"

It was as if a great sphere of light had sprung from somewhere and come hurling through, hurling through the night sky to pierce the Earth Mother directly in the center of their Gathering, through the symbols, as if cutting with a knife!

The Earth Mother shook. They felt it beneath their feet. They heard a rumbling. Even in their wonderings, they continued to emanate light.

From the very center where the hurling struck, the Earth Mother parted, first a little, then a little more and then a little more. Even through the shaking, they stood their ground.

Soon there was a noise. It was nearly the sound of the hissing of a snake, except it was louder. They thought, "It was louder." It came from the center where the opening was. From that center began to flow, slowly, thick blue essence. Thick, nearly as thick as nectar. Blue, it flowed outward from the Earth Mother.

It filled the circle, filling, but not going beyond. Nearly coming to touch their feet, and yet not quite. It flowed, and in the center it formed a cylinder of thick blue nectar essence. They looked upward to see, for it was three times taller than they. Thick blue nectar. Never had they seen such a thing before, ever, for never had there been on the Earth Mother such a thing before.

And even as they viewed it, there came from behind the top of the mountain a glowing of red, deep red. It was a glow that lit the sky with red.

They wondered, "What would this be? What would this be?" Even as they wondered, the one who remembered, the teacher, the two young ones and the villagers stood their ground and radiated light.

The red flowed, thick nectar, flowing nearly like a river. Over the top of the mountain it came, and just as it was to come upon them, it parted. It parted right at the blue cylinder and went around them.

So close it came, and yet it did not touch them. Thick red nectar, down it flowed over the edge and down the mountain, and even into the village. Red, it was. Still, the beings of light stood their ground.

From the top of the cylinder there seemed to come a beam of golden light. It went upward and upward until streams of light flowed and began to spin around and around. It became white, as if thick white nectar. Around and around it spun, as if it were weaving a dome over them all. And it did! A lighted dome formed over the blue cylinder and over those gathered around.

And then, as if they were a feather, they lifted upward. The beings within, even though they felt themselves moving, stood their ground, radiating. There were no thoughts. There were no feelings. Just light. Radiating. They spun around and around, a disc moving.

Soon it came to land upon the Earth Mother once again. Slightly, ever so slightly and gently, it settled in the golden field, in the center of the radiating symbols of light. They had been as beacons to it.

In the center of the great encampment of the People, it settled. In the center of the radiating symbols, it settled. In the center of the flowing light of the Gathering of the People, it settled.

Sounds came forth from the lighted dome and the Song of the Gathering was sung. Even from within the dome, the young one with the staff was standing there radiating light and singing the sound of the song. Lightly and clearly, the Song of the Gathering he sang.

As if it were a great white blossom, the dome began to part. It was as if the petals of the greatest radiating light blossom parted and flowed downward, revealing the circle of light of the beings within, all vibrating. The heart of the one with the staff, singing the song, swelled and filled with joy.

Upon the great blue cylinder he placed his staff, touching the tip of it and placing the other end directly upon the disc centered over his heart. The light radiated from the disc down through the staff and onto the blue cylinder. A ring of light surrounded the cylinder.

When he placed his staff once again beside his foot on the great Earth Mother, the cylinder began to part — just a little and then a little more. Stepping forward from the parting of the cylinder came a being, a blue being, vibrating lighted essence of blue. Stepping forward!

Those glowing so light and so white, the villagers and the three saw. They thought perhaps they had never before seen such beauty. As they were viewing the one, there came another stepping out of the cylinder of blue nectar. Essence of blue surrounded him as he stood in the strength of his being. Then another and another until there were, encircling the cylinder itself, twelve in number.

When they had completed standing, the Earth parted just a tiny crack and the remaining blue nectar flowed inward...not slowly and not quickly, it just seemed to flow inward. When it was completed, the great Earth Mother closed again.

The beings of blue walked outward, and in the walking they formed the patterns of their truth. They encircled the encampment until the great cocoons began to glow, and into them the blue beings did step and reside.

The beings of light in the center, those of the villagers, those of the three, laid themselves down on the petals of the white blossom of light.

The one, the one with the staff, stood exactly in the center of the Gathering and he sang the song, the Story, as if a lullaby he sang, that peace might be amongst them. And even as he sang softly the Story, he felt his grip tighten upon the staff and he felt the Old One within him. Even as his voice soared but a little, he remembered...everything.

And then, upon the Earth Mother came a shudder. For two, there were two now, two beings who resided upon the Earth Mother who remembered everything. Everything.

And the Council would meet, for even Level Red was flowing, and nothing from that depth had they recorded ever flowing without upon the great Earth Mother.

"It seems as though," she thought, "the Council will have to do something more than observe."

In the Gathering of the People, the union had begun.

Dear ones, the union has begun. Perhaps you have felt it at one time or another. Perhaps you have seen proof of it. Even with your doubts and concerns and your own feelings of hatreds, even with the slightness of all of that, the union has begun! For you are the People, you are the truths. And, my dear friends, from what level did you arrive?

CHAPTER FIFTEEN

The Warrior Enters

Upon the rising of the day of light, the Great Warrior and the Old One, Mother of her People, and the Old One, Father of his People, and his People did rise.

Hallowed be the ground upon which they have lain.

Without glancing back, first one and then another began the journey, stepping inward, into the opening of the Great Mother, who parted herself. Inward they went through the caverns.

Even as they turned around the great corridor, their way was lighted and their viewing adjusted to the dimness of light. They continued inward, breathing the breath of praise for the great Earth Mother, that she would invite them inward.

When the last had stepped within the corridor and around the turn, the opening closed, that none else might enter the journey within.

THREE MESSAGES

The First Message

There comes upon this Earth Mother another gathering which occurs in the period of once every one thousand years. Within this gathering are those who assist in determining the releasing of scientific data, truth in principles which would assist the natural flow of living of those peoples residing upon the planet called Earth.

There have been residing upon this planet those beings who, in their expanded consciousness, have been able to enter the dimensions wherein reside portions of these truths.

It is for the betterment of the Earth and the betterment of the universe that the truths reside within dimensions accessible to those who have integrated their consciousnesses. And yet, there have been those who have entered and have been able to gather certain truths and return, truths believed to be used for the betterment of the planet and the universe. Yet the remaining consciousness of certain beings upon this planet called Earth have, at times, turned the truths toward their own designs.

This has been and will be ever more the nature of physicality. However, it is for this reason that the truths reside within the dimensions of which we have spoken.

Then there comes upon this time, another gathering, the Gathering of which we are speaking. This Gathering of beings fulfills the purpose of vibrating within the scientific truths that they might be made whole.

When we say, "It is the time of the Gathering," we are speaking of more than we realize you could have recognized, for it is the Gathering.

On this planet called Earth, there have been, periodically, gatherings of the People. On this planet called Earth, there have been gatherings of those who reside in dimensions unknown to the beings inhabiting the planet called Earth. For there are many who reside within and without this grand, grand planet. And when we speak of the Gathering, then we would say: In all the history of time, even that which has not been recorded upon the records available in this physicality and even that which has been recorded also in those dimensions of expansiveness of time, never once has there been this Gathering.

For in the natural rhythm of events, it has come that this Gathering, this Gathering of which we have been speaking, is the Gathering of many, many.

There have been several considerations within the Gathering of beings residing in the purpose of vibrating the wholeness of truth of scientific data.

One consideration has been that the information presented in the total consciousness of the planet would provide great confusion. For it is a time of turning from believed, proven truths to wholeness.

Therefore, through all considerations, it has been decided that there would be a releasing of the truths themselves, that they might, in this physicality, take form and present themselves.

In this manner, then, there would be possibilities of discovery of truths in direct proportion to the expansiveness of consciousness toward the whole.

Therefore, there would be presented in several locations upon the planet called Earth, forms demonstrating wholeness of truth. Strange though these forms may appear, and strange though the workings of these forms may appear, it would provide the Earthly dimension with the opportunity of releasing believed truths and exploring wholeness.

For, if there would be a form presented before you which could demonstrate matter forming and disforming in a manner that would allow you to see the truth as it occurs, then there would be less confusion and less tendency to cling to previously useful beliefs of truths.

For, as the Gatherings do come together, there would be raised vibrations throughout this entire planet called Earth. These truths would assist in the understanding of what would be occurring upon this planet called Earth.

The Second Message

Residing upon our planet are many beings, different forms they take, all residing upon our planet. During the Great Breath of the universe, there comes change – the breathing in and the breathing out. When the universe breathes in, that which was without enters inward. And when the universe breathes out, that which was inward resides without.

At such a time there are few who can observe this occurrence. Once in a millennium does it occur. Then, on our planet, we who reside within, prepare. For in observing, we have recognized the time of change approaching when we who reside within would then reside without, that we who live within would flow to without, carried upon the breathing outward of the universe; and those who reside without then would flow within upon the breathing in of the universe.

This has been the natural flowing of our planet. There are those who observe, few though they be, who recognize this rhythm. We prepare ourselves for the change. Those of us who flow upon the breath experience the change as if we were but breathing. Yet when we breathe the breath once, we are breathing from within our planet. And then, in the next moment, we are without.

Few though we be, observers, we present ourselves that you might be knowing of this rhythm. Those who are unable as yet to be observers experience the change as if they were sleeping and awaken within a dream. And there they reside – it appears to them – within their dream.

Within every change there are those who awaken and begin to remember. These, then, become observers. This occurs on our planet, and we speak with you from within, wherein we reside. And yet, the change approaches.

That you might know, our planet is called Earth.

The Third Message

Then upon the great Earth Mother did come gatherings.

Even each presenting a truth did grow, and there came from one gathering and then another those who remembered, those who called themselves observers, those who called themselves the People, those who in a moment's breath change completely. Together they gather.

And even as we speak together, the gatherings continue. And even as we speak this tale, The Story of the People, *we can recognize those gatherings.*

Perhaps those gathering together radiate the truths. Perhaps we vibrate with them and feel the truths as we gather together, the People.

If you radiate the truths, then you are gathering together. If you resonate in one truth in one part of the Story of the People, then you are gathering together. Welcome home, the People, for you gather together. It is the time; none before have gathered together in this completion.

See it in your own eyes. See it in others. Feel it in your heart of hearts. Home. For we beckon you to come home, to remember...to come home.

When we are telling this tale, within the story we speak of all gatherings, that the truths might be known and presented, that those who have eyes can see, and those who have ears can hear. In this manner, then, there is the telling of this tale that you might understand more deeply the purpose for the manifestation of the truths in forms unfamiliar to you.

Oh People, when you feel yourself in the presence of the unknown, resonate. Rejoice! Sing the Song of Praise! For know you then that you have come upon the wholeness of truth. Allow yourself to merge, to experience the truth in totality. Yes, your beliefs will be turned away from you. And yet, the newness of the whole fills your being, resides within.

Herein, then, we speak these words:

Fear not for the change of the breath.

You have slept and awakened many times,

And those of your loved ones, too, have slept and awakened many times.

Fear not.

Those who awaken in the dream, then, are the People remembering who they are. Yes, in the story and also in your heart of hearts.

PART TWO
The One

CHAPTER SIXTEEN

It Was as if He were Stepping from a Great Green Forest

It wasn't the sweeping hot winds, nor their feet sinking into the dry sands with every step; neither was it the empty horizon that filled their minds as they crossed the pale expanse. That He had actually asked them to come with Him transformed an arduous journey into a delightful dance. In fact, they would follow Him anywhere, and even though He had motioned them to walk at His side, the space between them was filled with deep reverence. Their minds were filled with Him, for He was "The One."

They were changed a little right from the very first moment that He came amongst them. A type of joy, perhaps it was hope that they felt. Relieved from the burdens of their living, even though they wouldn't have called their lives so at the time, they felt uplifted in mind, heart and soul. Traveling together with Him now, there were many who thought in their minds back to the time when He had first come to them....

It was as if He were stepping from a great green forest. In their homeland not many trees survived, only rocks, a few shrubberies and roots. Yet, when He appeared, it was as if He brought the waterfalls of hope upon His shoulders. Upon His shoulders was a great urn which He carried as He walked. He reached them as they were digging into the Earth finding roots, the dust blowing upon them. 'Twas in the very center of the daylight when His presence came.

Even before He spoke, they loved Him and didn't know why. No strangers ever came to them, they were simply people of themselves until The One. He smiled upon them as if He were their father and they the children, even though many were quite aged. Still, even the aged felt as if they were one of his children, so great was He as He came amongst them. Placing before them the great urn, with one wave of His hand, He motioned them to come, and although they never would have, this time they did. They came, slowly, yet directly.

When they had gathered around in the number of three hands, He opened the urn and there within were sweet, cool waters. He dipped a tiny cup into the urn as they watched.

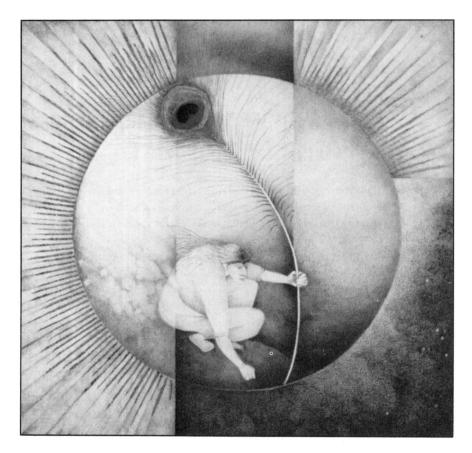

New Beginnings

"The women knew he was The One for whom they had waited. Their heritage spoke of a tale...of One who would come amongst them. Even in the weaving on the floor, which they had woven with their own hands, there was the story of his coming."

Each one remembered with relish the beginning of this time together with Him.

Not even a drop did he partake first, but offered the cup to them. They, standing there, dust upon their beings, parched lips and tongues, had been digging, digging for roots. He reached out that tiny cup to one who stepped forward and took it in his hand. The coolness of the cup itself startled him. Then to his lips he placed the brim and allowed cool sweet water to trickle inward.

The One refilled the cup and offered it to him again! "But what of the others?" he motioned. The One motioned him to drink it down, and this he did. He felt the coolness enter his being, he felt the sweet nectar enter his being and spread through his limbs, and he breathed a deep sigh of relief.

Then he dipped the cup into the urn, and even as he did, thought, "How dare I do this?" Yet, he was doing it. He passed the cup to his friend, and then to each one, all drinking their fill of the sweet water, cool, clear and fulfilling.

And The One, The One.

Even as they thought of the first moment they drank the water with Him — for after they had had their fill, then He dipped the cup and He too drank of the water — even as they thought back to the very first time, they spoke in their minds to each other with great love for The One, The One who came amongst them.

Then He lifted the urn again upon His broad shoulder and began to walk. Quickly, they gathered what few roots they had uncovered, placed them in their satchels and followed Him.

Of course they knew, even as He stepped upon the parched path, that He was going toward their tiny village. It took three of their steps to follow one of His long strides. Indeed, as they looked upon Him, they looked upward. He was three of their size. And yet, even as they hurried to keep pace with the long strides, they knew they loved Him.

'Round the rocks He went and then into their tiny village. They lived amongst the rocks, the largest one providing shade for them during that time of the day. Under one of the great rocks, He again placed down the urn.

The women and children had retreated into the caves to enjoy the coolness there and it was the tiny children who peeked out first. Who was this? Only when their curious eyes saw their fathers and friends walking behind the stranger did they creep forward a little more.

At this, the hottest time of the day, the men usually returned with the roots, roots they would prepare for nourishment. The women came to greet them and stepping from the cave, they saw The One. It seemed as if He were a towering rock. The men of their village motioned them to come closer. Even as they did, their eyes maintained a gaze upon Him. His eyes were different from theirs. The women noticed. They gazed at His strong limbs. They were long, and His skin was different from theirs.

Under the shade of the great rock, The One removed a robe and placed it upon the Earth. He stood upon the large area it covered and motioned them to join Him there.

'Twas the children first, laughing as they did, and then the women. And yes, He placed the urn also in the shade. Yet before He opened the top of the urn, He reached into the robe upon his body, and when He brought His hand out and opened it..."What were those things in His hand?" the children thought.

He held them out. Golden nuggets, it seemed they were. He took one and placed it within His lips. They saw. He outstretched His arm again and they came forward.

One woman, even as she walked upon the desert sands, remembered this moment and her heart swelled with joy at the memory.

She stepped forward, took one golden nugget and placed it between her lips and inward upon her tongue. She felt the coolness of mind. It was as if the dust of the Earth that had been covering her being were blown free. It was as if those pieces of Earth remaining in her hair were blown free. It was as if there were coolness of light within her mind.

She looked upon The One with wonder. He motioned again for her to take another. She thought, "What of the others?" Still He motioned again, and she did partake again and again. It was as if there were a waterfall flowing within her.

Even as she took one from his hand and gave it to her friend, she was thinking, "Dare I do this?" and yet she did. Another and another had their fill. Again He reached his hand into his robe, and again were more nuggets.

She gave to one child and the child came toward Him reaching, reaching upward, reaching. The One settled down upon the robe and sitting, He opened his hand to the child. The child took one and then another. And the other children, numbering six, each slowly took one and then another. His hand was so large, much greater than theirs, and yet they all came forward until all had had their fill.

Yes, then He opened the urn and passed amongst them cool, sweet water, and they drank their fill. Cool nectar flowed throughout their being and they rejoiced.

They didn't know His name nor where He came from, yet they took His hand and guided Him toward the cave wherein they dwelled during this time of day. Even as He walked within, His presence seemed to light the cave a little.

There, upon the floor of the cave, was a great woven covering. Here they brought Him to lie down and from the urns in the back of the cave, the women brought vials of oil and they filled His hair. In the center of His hands, they placed oil. Upon His feet, they placed oil. And He did be, reclined, for three days and three nights.

The women knew He was The One for whom they had waited. Their heritage spoke of a tale, of One who would come amongst them. Even in the weaving on the floor, which they had woven with their own hands, there was the story of His coming. Their hearts rejoiced in celebration of the fulfillment of the story.

On the fourth day, He rose and began to sing songs. Sounds filled their cavern, going outward across the sands, and they all gathered 'round. He spoke with them. Never before had they heard such words. His voice was deep and resonant. As He spoke, it seemed that they knew what He was saying and they wondered how He could speak the words they had never heard and yet it appeared they knew what He was saying.

As He spoke, they heard their own tale that those before them had told. For three days and three nights He spoke with them, providing nourishment so that they would not go to dig for roots, but stay and hear. From the great urn, all dipped the cup and allowed the cool, sweet water to trickle into their beings.

On the seventh day, He stood and walked outward, motioning them to remain. He walked toward the great sands. With their beings they called to Him, for they had grown to enjoy His love, His presence.

As He was stepping, He turned and spoke with them saying, "When you believe I will never return, then I will be here. I will return." They watched as His great being crossed the sands.

For a time they watched, as if watching the spot where they last saw Him would perhaps bring sight of His return. Day after day, they watched. And yet, He did not return.

The men continued to gather roots and the women continued to sing the songs, the songs that He sang, The One. The urn remained. It never seemed to empty. Each time they opened the urn, it was filled to the brim.

As the days numbered onward, even though they drank the cool, sweet water, it was He they longed for. They ached for His presence again. And just when they thought they would never see Him again, He appeared.

They didn't see Him coming. Perhaps they had ceased watching the great sands, looking for His approach. And there He was, standing amongst them. They gathered about like children bursting with joy.

"Here I will be with you," He said, "and then I will go away once more. Just when you think you would grow old before you see me again, I will return." They gazed upon Him and only knew that they loved His being. "Here then," He said, "I will remain with you."

Their days were filled with joy. Great stories He told them, stories of others, other peoples, other villages. One morn when they awakened, there were great piles of robes, a gift for them.

Another morn when they awakened, He beckoned them to come and they followed. There, amongst the rocks, not too distant from their village, He pointed. As He pointed to the opening near the top, there appeared a trickle...just a little, and then a little more, and then a little more. There appeared to be sweet, cool water flowing.

They remarked amongst themselves and walked closer to see. Yes, flowing from the opening was cool, sweet water. Soon the flowing came to be a waterfall, soft and gentle.

He motioned them to go forward and they did, and to go forward more and they did. He lifted the hems of His robes and placed his feet in the water. They laughed.

It was flowing, first a little and then as a river, small, yet flowing. He placed His feet in the water and they too did. He walked through the water to the soft waterfall and there He removed His robes and stood right in the waterfall!

He called them to Him. Hesitantly they came, first one and then another. Soon they were all standing under the soft waterfall, feeling it fall upon them. The dust of the great sands fell from them. They felt the coolness and rejoiced.

All day they stayed, laughing, playing, rejoicing. Then He placed His robes again upon His great being and returned to the cavern.

The waterfall continued to flow. It filled the crevasses and soon a pool began to form at the bottom of the great rocks. Each day they laughed and played together in the cool water. When they did, He would lean His head backward and laugh a deep laugh and they would turn and laugh with Him. Then He would sit at the edge of the pool and speak with them. Stories, unending stories it seemed He had. Stories that carried them far away.

One morn He called them to follow again and He brought them to a place on the other side of the great rocks. He pointed to the Earth. Six times He pointed, and in the six places sprang forward – "What was that?" they thought – sprang tiny trees. Before their eyes they grew and grew until they were greater than He.

Again He pointed to the trees and there, hanging from them was fruit. He went to the first tree and, plucking a fruit, gave it to them. It was large in their hands. From each tall tree he plucked a fruit, each one different in color, in taste and in size. They laughed and danced about the trees, and as they danced about The One, He leaned back His head and laughed a great deep laugh. They sat under the trees and as they ate the fruit, again He spoke with them of journeys He had made, places He had seen.

When in the evening the stars came upon them, He beckoned them and again they followed. As He pointed upward, there appeared a golden ball coming from the very sky upon which they gazed. It came closer and closer and soon, in the light of the darkness, the glowing golden ball appeared before them and rested itself upon the sands.

He pointed again and the golden ball spun 'round and 'round until it spun right into the sands and it was as if it had never been there at all. They wondered. And yet He gathered them about and embraced them and sang them songs, and they ceased to wonder.

There, upon the sands they rested, remembering the golden ball of light.

He stayed with them for one year and then one morn He gathered them about. They brought containers of fruit for nourishment and He smiled upon them and loved them. He spoke. "On the morrow, then I will not be with you. And yet, I will return. As I have, I will again. You would think perhaps you would become old before you see me again. When you think these thoughts, then I am with you again."

They embraced Him, some gathered together and sat upon Him and He embraced them. Then He sang them a song and the story of the song was the story of themselves from when He first came amongst them. He told them of themselves and of His love for them and of the joy.

Even as one dipped his little foot into the pool of water, just for the enjoyment of it, The One sang of the beauty of their beings when first they stood beneath the waterfall and of the beauty of their beings even as they sat about Him, and of the beauty of their beings even as they gathered the fruit. He sang of them and their light and their beauty.

From the great urn, He dipped the cup once again and they drank and ate fruit together. As they laid themselves down to rest, He also rested, and in the morn, when they awakened, even at the first light, He was not amongst them. They knew then He would return, for had He not once before? Had He not once before?

They gathered together and sang the Song of Return. And he did hear.

As they walked upon the sands, all of this they remembered. There He was, just a little ahead of them, walking with those great strides they knew and loved. Even the scent of His being they felt amongst them as they followed.

Blessings upon those receivers of this tale, your tale. As He speaks with the People, we speak with you. Deep love there is for you.

CHAPTER SEVENTEEN

Woven Reeds upon Their Feet

They followed Him as children would, not wondering where they were going, how they would live or what would be their nourishment or shelter.

As they walked, one amongst them remembered the words and the fulfillment of the words: "You will think you will become old before I return. On that day I would return." She thought to herself, "Those were my exact words." She had been standing atop the rocks at the beginning of the waterfall and looking outward, outward and seeing nothing but the sands in any direction....

She'd been facing the direction from where He'd come once before, and even though she was still young, she thought, "I'll be an old woman before He returns."

A bit startled, she had felt a hand upon her shoulder and turning...there He was. The sight of Him filled her. In the next breath He was sitting with her. She looked deep into His eyes and began to think, "Where is it that you go," but His presence was so filling that even the question slipped her mind. "You are here," she thought. "You are here!"

Together they stood under the coolness of the waterfall. Soon others came and their hearts were filled with the sight of Him. Without hesitation they too joined in the celebration of His return under the soft-falling waters.

Some had gathered fresh fruit and together they all sat and ate in silence. Then He beckoned them to come and sit under the great rock, upon the weaving where He had lain when He had first come amongst them.

Before He began speaking, one woman collected a vial from the cave and bringing it forward, she placed a little oil in each of her own palms. Then upon His forehead she placed her hands, anointing Him with oil, and they were together.

He pointed to the weaving upon which they sat and there they saw themselves together, walking. He spoke with them as He had previously, telling stories of journeys and other peoples. They heard the words.

Again He pointed to the weaving and there they saw themselves in number twice their own standing and again He spoke of other peoples.

She remembered how they had lain themselves down to rest, and even
though when her eyes were closed she saw Him still sitting there, never did she
wonder if He rested, but simply basked in the presence of His being. This she
remembered while walking in the sands.

He ceased walking and turned toward them, His great long arms stretching
outward. He pointed to the sands and before them sprang a tiny tree. It grew
before their eyes and soon it was tall enough to provide shade, in which they
rested.

Once again, reaching into His robes, he removed His hand and in it were tiny
golden nuggets. They each reached forward and took nourishment from His
hand. Three times He reached into His robe and pulled forth golden nuggets
for them.

When they were filled, He brought from his garment a tiny vial and placed
one drop of the elixir within upon one finger. They did the same as He and then
placed that finger within their mouths. It was as if the center of the flowers
burst forth within and their senses were filled.

Again from His garment he brought something forth. It appeared to be a
piece of wood. It was dark and rich with patterns. In the wood were holes. He
placed the wood to His lips and trickling forth came resonant sounds. He played
for them the Song of Nourishment and Resting and their beings were filled.

They rested for a time and when they stood together He pointed once again.
They turned to see where He was pointing. There was something there.
Walking closer, they found woven reeds. He showed them how to place them
upon their feet.

As they continued onward with the woven reeds upon their feet, they found
the walking upon the sands quite different, as if they remained atop! Like
children, they smiled and pointed to the things they were wearing upon their
feet. Yet when they continued with ease, one thought, "He takes care of
everything."

One glanced back to see where they had been sitting in the shade of the tree
only to see but sand there. He turned and continued onward with them. Still,
he wondered. One of them wondered.

As dusk came upon them, they thought to settle and at the thought it was as
if they came upon a vision. As they walked closer and closer, the vision became
larger and larger. There, provided for them, was a resting place. Woven reed,
once again they saw woven reed. They walked to the shelter and felt it, smelled
it, breathed the essence. Around on the sand were woven containers holding
fresh fruit.

Where they would lay themselves down was a woven covering. One woman
went closer to examine the pattern before she sat down. One picture of many
people together; it was the same as the weaving from their home, yet only one
picture. She saw.

Beyond the rushes growing in front of the shelter, sparkling fresh water invited them to part the green leaves and refresh themselves. There, in the water was woven reed, upon which they sat and bathed, laughing and playing in the joy of being.

Before they laid themselves down for rest, He spoke with them saying, "Here you will reside for three days. Then I will return." Even as they laid their heads down, when the last eyes were closed, He was gone.

On the morning of the first day, they found that a being much like themselves had entered the shelter at some time during the night. He lay there. His appearance was much like The One when he had first come amongst them. As he stirred a little, they approached him.

They placed a container of cool, sweet water and allowed it to trickle upon his lips. He stirred a little more. From a vial, one woman put oil upon his forehead and he stirred a little more. Another stroked his head, softly and gently. The woman placed oil in the palms of his hands. Again he moved.

Then they bathed his limbs and removed the scarce covering and bathed his being. Like their own, they placed a robe upon him and gently, ever so gently, lifted him and laid him down upon the woven covering. Still, as he lay there, he maintained his grasp upon the staff in his hand. None touched the staff.

On the morning of the second day, they found yet another being. "Came some time during the night," they thought, gathering around. They saw a woman, different from them, yet similar. This one was only two hands taller than they. She barely stirred. Upon her tattered robe, which barely covered her being, they saw woven threads — a golden symbol, round. They placed upon her a new robe and cared for her being. Only a little did she stir.

On the morning of the third day, they found amongst them yet another being. There on the woven reeds upon the water there lay another. They pulled the woven reeds to them. Never had they seen a being like this one. Blue he was, deep blue, and large, larger than they.

They pulled the woven reeds from the water and the woman with the vials of oil came. Upon his entire being she placed the oils until he was glistening, deep blue. Then upon him, too, they placed a robe.

They knew upon the rising of the morn of the next day He would return, for this he said to them: "Three days, and then I will return." Amongst them now were three new beings.

They nourished themselves and sang the Song of Peace, which He had taught them. Never once were the three beings without someone at their sides, caring, singing softly, caressing gently, ever so gently.

Even as they prepared for rest, the woman stirred a little. She said two words. The one with her heard. "The Council," she said. Gently, ever so gently, he caressed her forehead and her being and she settled again to rest.

There they lay and the one who wondered, before he slept, wondered again, "What will He do with these three? What will He say to us?" Even at the thought of Him, he was filled with joy and thought, "In the morn He will be here." Even as he settled to sleep, the joy permeated his entire being and he breathed the breath of sleep.

And it was the end of the third day.

Blessed are you who hear and receive this tale, for truly there cannot be telling of the tale when there are none to hear, to receive. Blessed are you.

CHAPTER EIGHTEEN

From the Sand He Pulled
a Great Blossom

The appearance of the three beings reminded some of a time long ago when, one by one, each of them had gathered at the place they called their home in the rocks. A few had no memory at all of their own arrival. To them, it was as if they had been there since birth. But there was one who remembered a time before he had come to that place, remembered the lush, rich green of the Earth Mother.

As they waited for The One, many reminisced within their own memories, for the three who had entered their encampment had come looking as battered and worn as they had been....

It had been a long journey for many, searching and searching in a barren land for just one other, feeling that there were others, somewhere. Where were the others? Then, like a magnet, finally, finally they felt themselves drawn and they followed. First one and then another and then another came to those rocks they called their home. They were nearly depleted, yet in finding each other felt a little replenished.

Seldom did they speak together of the past or their place of origin, refraining for the sake of those who couldn't remember. One or two could only be gathering and preparing roots. They had never been completely replenished. There were those, too, who could only observe, even as they lived together.

The one who remembered more kept his memories to himself. He remembered the lushness and even before the lushness, there was barren earth; and before that, there was lushness, and before that, barren earth, and before that, lushness. His memories went on and on.

And yet, as he brought his thoughts to this evening, while they slept, he wondered of the rest, the others. "Were they somewhere ahead of them? And The One...." It wasn't that he was surprised or astounded at the manner in which The One assisted them. Still, there was something about Him.

"No, no," he tried to sort his thoughts, "it's not even about The One. It's about the occurrences themselves." He remembered the trees springing up from the sands and the water flowing from the rocks. He couldn't yet figure it out. "How could it have happened that way? It was as if The One had turned the page and there were the trees and the water." Sleep beckoned him. "We'll see in the morning." He glanced around at his friends once more and then laid his head down, letting the thoughts slip away.

At the dawning of the fourth morn, The One stood in their encampment and viewed them all, barely stirring. In His arms He carried a child. It was as if their presence called to those sleeping, and soon one woman awakened. Even before opening her eyes, she knew He had returned and allowed the joy to fill her a moment longer. Then she saw Him and then the child and before she knew it, she was walking toward The One and outreaching her arms.

He place the child into her outreaching arms. The child gazed upon her and as he did, it was...it was as if she remembered...something....Yet had she actually experienced those pictures that came into her mind?

When she averted her gaze, the child placed his tiny hand upon her cheek. Looking again into his eyes, she found love, and even though it was a child in her arms, she felt as though he were an ancient wise one. He placed his other hand upon her other cheek and held her face. His love was strong. She felt it.

The others in the encampment began to stir and stretch their limbs and then see The One. He reached into his robes and pulled forth golden nuggets, calling them to rise and eat.

'Twas then that they saw the child and gathered about him. "Such a one," they thought, as they touched the tiny hand that reached out to them.

The One motioned to them and when they had gathered around, sitting together, He dipped His hands into the sands, almost as if He were digging, yet simply moving His hands in the sands. He looked at them as He began to remove His hands from the sands and they saw a blue ball of light. He held it out for them to see.

He reached into the sands again and pulled out a golden rod. They watched as He again reached into the sands and again pulled out something — this time a chalice. Again, and He pulled forth sparkling white crystalline. He continued until there were many things laid there upon the sands.

Their gaze remained upon Him as He then took each item one by one, and placed it between his hands. Each one returned to sand! He continued until the very last, even the blue ball of light, had become sand and all the things were gone.

Climbing down from the woman's arms, the child walked to the sand and began to move it to one side. From the sand he pulled a great blossom, and even as he turned to raise it to the woman whose arms had held him, fragrance filled them all.

It wasn't as if they were astounded; they simply watched, for The One had shown them many things, had told them many stories and had sung them many songs. He placed His head backward and laughed a deep laugh from within His great being, and before they knew it, they too were laughing.

He spoke with them again of themselves and of the journey they were making together, saying, "There are others." He stood and dipped the cup into the urn. They didn't remember bringing that urn, yet there it was. They each drank...except one.

He walked over to the sand where The One had placed His hands, and reaching inward, moved the sand around. He felt nothing there, nothing at all. The One saw him and while the others were filling themselves with water, went to him. Together, one hand in the other, they placed their hands in the sand and then in the memory of the one who had remembered everything, came a thought: a golden ball of light. Even as the thought came to his mind, he felt it forming in his hand. Together they removed their hands from the sands and there it was — the golden ball of light!

He looked at it and then at The One. Taking his own hands, he placed them together and the ball became sand once again. Without hesitation, he reached his own hand into the sand and again came thought of the golden ball of light. Yes! He felt it form in his hand! He removed his hand from the sand and there it was! There it was in his hand. Again he placed his hands together and it became sand. He looked at The One. They viewed each other, for none of the others had seen this.

None of the others, for their attention was drawn to the woman who had arrived on the third night. She stirred a little, barely able to wonder where she was. She remembered just a little from the previous evening. Loving hands had stroked her being.

Feeling the fresh garment on her body, her eyes searched for the old tattered one. It was beside her and her shaking hand held barely enough strength to reached out for the emblem. Closing a weak grasp upon the golden emblem, she whispered again, "The Council."

One of them brought a cup and allowed the cool water to trickle across her swollen lips. Still she was unable to rise and soon closed her eyes again to rest, to sleep. The One came to her and from His garment brought forth a small, round black berry between His fingers and placed it to her lips. As He pressed the berry, the nectar flowed onto her lips and trickled within, and even as she rested, she felt a tiny drop of nourishment enter her being.

He went to the boy who still held the staff in his hands, the one who had arrived upon the second day, and placed a berry on his lips. As He pressed, the nectar trickled forth into the boy. Still he remained unmoving.

Gathering those traveling with Him together, and the child, The One sang the Song of Nourishment. Together they sat around the three who had arrived so depleted and softly sang the songs. This they did on the fourth day and very little more.

For three more days they cared for those three, anointing them with oil and wrapping their sore, cracked feet. Each day The One placed a berry at their lips and pressed the nectar into their being. Then He said, "On the morn, we would begin again."

They prepared a bed upon which they would lay those three who could not yet walk of themselves. Even though they felt joy to be with The One, there was concern for these others amongst them. Some had remembered when they themselves had ever so slowly regained their strength, not yet vitality, simply strength, a little at a time. He felt their troubled minds and outstretched His arms and sang them the Song of Praise for who they were, what they had done together, of their journey, of their caring. He sang the Song of Peace and it filled their beings. That evening they rested in peace.

While they were resting, He went to the one with the staff and quietly pulled aside his garment. There upon the young body was a mark, a mark where perhaps a disc had lain. He saw and then closed the garment. Stroking the boy's head, The One spoke softly, saying, "Return gently, return slowly, my dear one." Even as the boy slept, He pressed a berry to his lips and watched the nectar flow inward.

Just The One and the child remained awake through the night. As they gazed upon each other, between them formed a light, a tiny glowing that filled the encampment, covering them all with peace, with deep love and with nourishment.

Are you not like them, dear ones, trying to remember, and yet a little unable? Yes, you see? The Story of the People is your story, you are the People, and as The One comes and speaks with them of their heritage, so we come amongst you and tell this tale of your heritage, that you might know.

Fear not for what you call destruction. We will always be ready to place the berry between our fingers and place it upon your lips and squeeze the berry that the nectar might enter, that you might be nourished. Always.

The door that has been closed to you is open. Were you not as a child, saying, "I have many questions," wanting to know, "What am I doing here? Why am I here? What is my purpose? Where is my home? Who are these people around me? Some feel like my family, and others do not. At times I feel lost and yet at times I feel that I am on the journey. To where, I'm not quite sure and yet I know I am."

See yourself? Even the People in the story are not quite remembering. You are perfect. As we breathe the breath of peace within them, then the breath of peace flows within you, if you will allow it to.

The time is at hand when the dust will be blown away and the cool, clear water will wash your being. You will be nourished and filled and within your heart of hearts will be rejoicing even without knowing why. For the time is at hand that the People would raise themselves from the dust and begin the journey to who they are.

Fear not for what you term to be survival. Every plan is of the past. Take heart, dear ones. Union is at hand, and just as The One says to the beloved, "Slowly and gently return," we say unto you, that is the purpose of the story: slowly and gently, hearing your heritage and also knowing, words take form.

You are more found than you have ever been lost before.

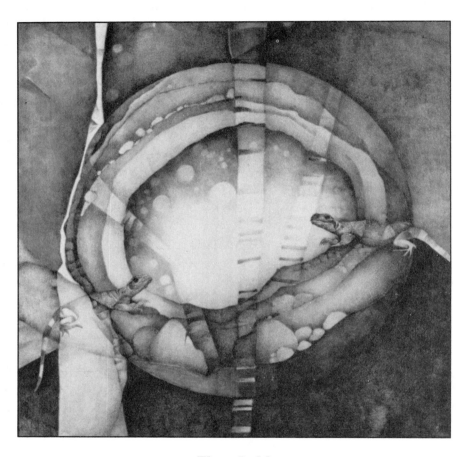

Threshold

"In the mountain, before their eyes, an opening parted."

CHAPTER NINETEEN

She Sang Them the Song, Preparing Them

Even though they continued day after day, because they basked so in His love and in the presence of His being, each day was filled with joy. Even unto the twenty-first day, they carried the three who barely stirred, and still The One continued to nourish them.

On this, the twenty-first evening, when they gathered about, encircling Him, they laid the three close beside them so that they would be continually in their presence. "On the morn," He said, "we will make yet another journey. And I am with you. In this evening we will sing the Songs of Praise for these sands that have borne us thus far."

They sang the song of the rocks of their home shelter and they sang the song of the roots. They sang the Song of the Gifts The One had bestowed upon them and the Song of Praise of the journey. Lastly, they sang the Song of Praise of the three who had come amongst them.

Then one woman stepped before Him and to The One she sang the Song of Praise of His presence amongst them, and their hearts did soar in hearing the words of their own hearts, singing the Song of Praise of Him amongst them. He received their Song of Praise and they were together.

From His robe, He brought forth this time something different. Green, they were, glowing green nuggets. They lighted His hand and He gave one to each of them. Following His example, they placed the green nugget upon their lips and then into their mouths. Again and again they did, until each had eaten three and held a fourth in his own hand.

"When you first awaken in the morn," He said, "eat this fourth one."

The one who had wondered previously and who had placed his hands in the sands wondered again, "What is the purpose of this?" He was nearly hiding his wondering when he glanced up to see — yes — The One gazing upon him with all His love.

He spoke with them, saying, "On the morrow we will take another journey together and then you will know much more than you know now." He placed his large hand upon the shoulder and the head of the one who wondered and the love flowed between them.

This time when they rested, they were simply upon the sands, and as they breathed deeply He sang, as He had before, the Song of the Others.

When they awakened in the morn, they placed the fourth green glowing nugget in their mouths. It wasn't until they rose that they saw it. It was as if it had risen up from the sands. There before them stood a grand mountain.

They looked around. "Where was He?" It was then that they heard His deep laughter and then another laughter, not quite as deep as The One, yet deep laughter.

There they spotted them, at the foot of the mountain. There was the boy with the staff in his hand and The One and they both were leaning their heads backward and laughing a deep laugh. Then they also saw standing with them with her long golden hair flowing, the woman who had come amongst them on the second morn. As they looked they saw the being with the deep blue skin, even in the morn they could see. He had removed the robe they had so gently placed upon his being. There he was. There they all were!

As if The One knew they were looking, He turned toward them and in a few strides came upon them. He was glowing. Never before had they seen him so filled with joy! "Come," He said. "Come! Let us begin a new journey."

Where they walked, the sands became a path for their feet to easily step upon. As they journeyed up the rise toward the mountain, on either side of the path were little green bushes, and then a tree, and then, as they began the incline, a few more trees. They walked with ease, as if His very breath carried them forward. To be with Him was to be without effort.

As they placed their feet upon the mountain itself, they felt a surge of strength flow within them. Still they neither paused nor spoke between them, but continued upward. The rock of the mountain was neither warm nor cold, was neither sharp nor smooth. It simply was the mountain and the rocks thereon.

Soon they were at the place where they had seen Him with the three, and when they arrived, the three stood before them and sang the Song of Praise to the People who had bathed them, placed oils upon them and placed robes upon their beings. For the People who had cared for them gently, ever so gently, and who had carried them on this journey.

As the People heard the songs from the three, they felt a flowing as if of a waterfall, and nourishment as if from the fruit of the trees.

"Come," The One called to them. "Come." They all went forward and in the mountain before their eyes, an opening parted. As He placed one foot inward, again He said, "Come!"

The three motioned for them to go first. "Go along!" And this they did, stepping into the mountain itself. What appeared to be dark was light and they saw a glowing coming from themselves. The further into the mountain they stepped, the greater was their glowing.

They looked at themselves and at each other, holding up their arms and seeing the green glowing. The One, who was glowing white, called, "Come!" They followed Him into the mountain.

The three also followed. First the woman and the boy with the white glowing staff and last, stepping behind them all, was the dark blue being, emanating blue. Thusly they journeyed into the mountain.

They rested three times, laying themselves down, and each time upon rising they heard Him calling them to come. Inward and inward they traveled and even though there appeared to be darkness around them, there was light!

When they gathered together for nourishment, the woman with golden flowing hair came amongst them and sang a song of other beings who loved them, of beings who knew them well and who loved them.

In her sweet voice, they found comfort that there really were others. She spoke of the caring, of the gentleness and of the strength of the others. At length she sang them this song, preparing them for the next part of their journey. Then when she had finished and they had received nourishment, they continued onward, following Him and His words: "Come, come." They did love Him.

Then there came before them two pulsating entryways. Pulsating. One moment they were there before their eyes, and then the next moment they were not, appearing and disappearing. When The One approached one entryway, the light from His being lighted the way and they saw a swirling vortex in the entryway, as if a great wind had come and begun to swirl.

He showed them, placing His great arm and hand into the entryway. It seemed to disappear. And yet, when He brought it back, there it was. Again, He showed them, and without a hint, He stepped into the swirling and nearly completely disappeared — except for His one hand, reaching out toward them.

"Come!" They heard His familiar words. "Come!" One took His great hand and then another took the hand of that one, and another took the hand of that one, and soon, each of them holding each other's hand, they walked, following Him into the swirling vortex.

It was as if the ones before them stepped into the swirling and simply disappeared! Yet each one continued until the last, and then the boy with the staff, and then the woman.

When all else had entered the swirling, the dark blue being came to the two entryways. He motioned, moving his arm around and around and the two entryways came together as if they were one. The swirling increased and increased until he stepped inward as had the others. When the last part of his being had entered, then there was no entryway, no path, and there was no mountain...only sand.

The Land Within

"They simply viewed the great expanse. Here and there it appeared as though there were a mountain rising, and valleys, and waterfalls...the Land Within."

Blessed be the ones who gather together in the telling of this tale, for then there would be the telling of the telling, and then the telling of the telling of the telling. And soon the story would be taking form, for when those hear the story and are truly awakened, then they are the story, as are you, dear ones. Thusly then, the light is spread. Thusly then, the word is heard. Thusly then, the word is spoken again and again. Thusly then, we awaken to who we are: the People!

Never fear for who you are and the journey upon which you ride.

CHAPTER TWENTY

For Some, the Land Within Was Quite Different

For some, the Land Within was quite different. Where there had been under their feet sand and sand and more sand and where the wind had blown in their hair sand and sand and more sand and where they had dug for roots in sand and more sand, now there was lushness.

They had experienced a little of this lushness as The One had gradually transformed their place under the rocks. Yet, here was green. Here was water. Here was the scent of many. Here it was quite different for some.

For others, the Land Within rekindled memories of times before and their hearts embraced the green growth and soared with the tall trees and expanded with the sweet scent of blossoms in the air. For others, it appeared strangely familiar.

There, as they looked ahead of them, down into the valley, they saw the woman who had come in the night, whom they had cared for, her long, long light hair flowing as she walked ahead of them. It was as if she followed a path through the lushness, through the large green leaves. As she turned and looked back to them, they saw that she had placed on her robe the golden emblem she had clutched tightly once before. She had arranged her robe differently, turning it this way and that way, and crossing it over her shoulders, one bare and one covered.

Smiling toward them, she motioned and waved at the same time, as if she were going off upon her own journey, and indeed she was. For she entered the Land Within through the green lushness and even as she walked, she caressed the tiny shrubberies and embraced the trees. In her eye, a tear of joy formed for the joy of being.

She came upon a small pond and stopped for a moment to dip her slender hand into the water. And cupping it, she brought a little to her lips and she sipped the water. It flowed within her being and she recognized it. She knew the taste and the feel of this water, and she rejoiced again.

As she walked, she looked upward and upward. "Was it the walls?" she silently questioned. Then she saw it, a grand great structure built into the wall. It was as if a palace towered above her. "I wonder if they're there. I wonder if I'll find them there," she whispered to herself.

As she continued on the soft path beneath her feet, a tiny flying bird came near her. "So tiny and such a long beak," she thought. She held out her hand and there he sat and viewed her.

"Yes," she thought as she looked about in the great, grand expanse of the Land Within, "perhaps I'll find them there."

The others still stood and looked about. They hadn't really moved from the spot where they had entered the Land Within. They simply viewed the great expanse. Here and there it appeared as though there were a little mountain rising, and valleys and waterfalls. And yes, there, up at the top, seemed to be a great structure, a palace, carved right into the wall.

They looked further and further. It was as if the entire Land Within were lighted by the sun — except that they were truly within, and yet it was lighted and they felt the warmth upon them!

One of them who had no memories except of the sands, knelt down and felt the life within the Land. He pulled away part of it and crushed it in his hand and felt it and smelled it. It was moist and alive. It smelled rich. It was dark. "It is wonderful," he thought, "wonderful!"

There was green growing beside him and he reached out and touched it with his fingers. It felt soft and it too was alive. Greenness growing so close to the land, barely a breath away from the land it grew. He saw the roots going into the land.

There were no memories rekindled for him. Each place upon which his eyes gazed was a great discovery, and yet he could not bring himself to move forward. He simply gazed into the flowing of the Land Within, the great expanse, the light and the colors, the fragrances.

The one who had arrived on the reeds in the waters, the one with the skin of deep dark blue, stepped forward. They knew he wasn't waving goodbye but was simply going off a little way to discover what he would discover. His moving forth was different from the woman's. He stepped between the bushes and the trees and, bending his body here and there, soon was beyond the sight of their eyes. As he left them behind a little, he stood in the full strength of his being, stretching his limbs. Stretching himself to see over the tops of the bushes, he saw more and more plants growing and felt their moisture even as he touched them. It was then that he saw it.

It was another! It was another as he! Seemingly walking around and upward, as though there were a walking path upward, winding around that little mountain. And another! He was sure this time that he saw another. Yet, he didn't run to them. He simply watched. He felt the hand upon his shoulder even as he watched, and there The One stood. He felt great comfort with The One and yet great excitement in his heart of hearts for seeing — surely he had seen....

The One motioned him to return with Him. As they walked together, the being of deep dark blue turned to glance once more over his shoulder. He was sure he had seen them. Breathing deeply, he returned with The One.

Those beings whom He had gathered together from the rocks and who had traveled upon the sands, whom He had spoken stories to and sung songs to, whom He loved so dearly, those beings gathered about Him. Their green glowing had begun to diminish and they could see but a slight glimmer here or there.

The light around them remained as bright as ever. Truly, it was as if they were in the light of day, yet they were in the Land Within.

He spoke with them and they heard His words. "Here then," He said, "we shall reside. Here then, will be our home of homes. Here then, we can play and be. Here then, you can thrive. Here then, you will meet the others of whom I have been speaking. Here then, you may begin anew.

"And yet, there will be the time when I will come amongst you and beckon you to follow once again, and know you that some will follow and some will remain."

All thought deep in their heart of hearts that they did love Him and would always be with Him. Wherever He beckoned them to go, they would surely go. Yet he was saying that when he beckoned them, they would stay. "No," they thought, "that could not be."

Still He smiled upon them and said, "Yes. Some will remain and some will come. And yet, that is in the time of coming. Here we will be together."

They gazed upon Him and wondered. This time He did not reach into his robes and pull out golden nuggets of nourishment. This time He said, "Come here," and He showed them bushes and upon the bushes were berries just like the berries He had pressed to the lips of the others. He said, "Here. Fill yourselves."

Slowly, ever so slowly, they stepped forward, not out of fear, but simply in enjoying entering the Land Within. Yes, they did step forward and pick the berries with their fingers and place them to their lips and taste the sweet nectar. More and more they picked and ate, and He smiled upon them.

Even as the woman held the child, she picked the berries. The child turned his gaze upon The One and light formed between them. The boy with the staff saw and even at a moment's notice, stepped between the two, the child and The One, and into the center of the light. He felt it in his being. He knew it. He was familiar with this light! The word "home" resounded within and looking at The One and at the child, he stepped outward from the center a little.

Then once again, there were the three. It appeared that only these three saw and experienced this communion in light, for the others had turned away and were still eating berries. Even the woman holding the child did not see. Yet far above, in that great structure, there was one looking downward.

And he said to the others, "They are here. At last, they are here."

The One felt their words. "Yes," He thought, "we are here at last."

When they had finished with the berries, more of the Land Within called to them. They heard the trickling of water and wondered if it was like the waterfall The One had brought to them. They walked onward just a little, toward the sound. They did come upon water, but it was quite unlike a waterfall. It was as if a hole were in the side of a great rock and outward poured a stream of water. It trickled downward, downward, downward, downward to them. They reached out their arms and hands and felt the water. They brought it to their lips and tasted it. It was quite familiar. It was quite familiar, like the cool, sweet water from the urn. The urn.

There were those who, in tasting and recognizing the familiarity, thought back to when The One had come amongst them and of the things He had done. They turned to gaze upon Him and yes, there He was, ever at their side, smiling upon them.

They continued onward, downward, inward, into the Land Within, following the soft path, moisture everywhere. Downward and inward they went, into the Land Within.

They came upon a clearing, a golden field. It appeared that there might be others there. They wondered, "Are these the ones of whom He spoke with us?" They leaned forward to see.

Yet they only saw a deep golden field shaped like a large bowl. The land seemed to be cut away and there were places where they might walk and go deeper still. The One called to them, "Come along, come this way."

They went around the deep bowl of the field, still looking down toward the clearing. As they continued they saw, as if on the side of the mountain, a being waving, waving both arms. It was there they were going.

They continued until He stopped and said, "Here," motioning them to sit and rest as He did. Even though the darkness was not upon them, it was the time for resting and they laid themselves down together.

When they had all closed their eyes in sleep, then the child viewed The One and the boy with the staff, and again the light formed among them. The one with skin of dark deep blue saw. And when the child laid his head down to rest, and the boy with the staff, then the one of blue and The One remained together.

Softly, The One sang the Song of Praise for these beings, caressing them with his words.

In this manner they stayed resting there, and throughout the Land Within there was felt a flowing through the essence, a newness of beings. Those who resided there knew others had come and they sang the Song of Rejoicing within their hearts, for their numbers had grown.

They had been few at first. Quite few. Even when they had gathered together three or four in number, they had felt that they could perhaps live in this strange yet wonderful Land Within. Then they had come upon three or four more, and three or four more, and they gathered together to make for themselves a regular rhythm of living.

Then, as one journeyed further inward, exploring deep within the Land Within and coming back, he had spoken with them: "There are others." Some had traversed with him and others had remained. In this manner, different gatherings of beings began a new way in this strange and wonderful Land Within.

Those above in the great palace saw. They thought that they knew all, for they viewed everything and felt everything. And yet, The One had returned.

The glowing of the Land Within changed a little. They would learn about this the longer they were here. As did the others, they would learn. The lighting changed in the Land Within. At times it was bright as if the light of day, at times it was glowing, glowing green, almost as they were when they had walked through the caverns and come here. At times there was a glowing of red. And once, only once since they had been there, there was a glowing of blue.

Now there was a glowing of a little red, yet they were resting and didn't know it. Soon they would, though, for within this great land, there were many journeys to come. Even in the resting, there were those hearts who ached for regular living, for the rhythm within their lives. Those would be the ones who would remain.

All of this The One knew and much, much more. Much more. Softly, again He sang the Song of Praise for the Land Within. Then, though none other did hear, He sang the Song of Praise of His own journey. He sang the Song of Praise for Himself and for His own journey and His own being — for The One.

Even before He allowed himself to rest a little, he thought, "Only these remain." He thought of them all in the Land Within, a few here and a few there and a few more over there. Some had been here for quite some time. This He knew and much, much, much more.

He breathed a breath of nourishment into the Land Within and then He, too, rested His being. His was a resting of peace.

From the Land Within, we do breathe upon you the breath of peace. Blessed be those who join in this journey simply by hearing the telling of this tale.

CHAPTER TWENTY-ONE

Therein, He Saw the Great Shells

In the Land Within live many beings. There are those who remain even though the breath of the Earth Mother breathes inward and outward, carrying her people inward and outward. There are several places where those who remain reside: a few live in the great palace where they create worlds, where they observe worlds, where they assist those residing in other worlds, and where they maintain the balance of the Land Within.

Others who remain in the Land Within live in other locations. Four in number reside alone, each maintaining the work: one maintaining writings, another maintaining songs, another maintaining beauteous forms. These three maintain, lest the heritage of the beings be lost.

The fourth is the brother of The One. Very much alike are they, their statures, maintaining the dignity of all beings, are quite the same. The love, deep from the heart of hearts, is the same. Yet the brother lives in solitude and dwells atop the cliffs. None come to his dwelling except perhaps the birds, and they are very few. He travels atop the trees and within the caves. As with The One, he knows all of the Land Within and of all of those inhabiting the Land Within and much more.

He bears the color of the earth, red. His hair and long beard and even the hair on his arms, red. One might think that he had become the color of his cave, yet he is as he is.

On this day he felt his brother's return. The One. It was good to feel his presence, yet he knew that his brother would be continuing with this last group for a bit longer, assisting them to acclimate to the Land Within.

Then perhaps he and his brother could stand atop the stars once again and enter their own adventure. "Perhaps," he thought, "perhaps." For he yearned for adventure and his yearning filled his entire being.

He had been across the galaxies and back. He had danced the dance of the stars. He had held the planets in his hands. He had visited the worlds beyond the worlds. He had met with the forces of dissemination and stood his ground. Of all the adventures he had experienced, still he returned to this Land Within.

Here was peace for his soul. Here was balance for his spirit. Here was fulfillment for his being.

As he looked down from the edge of the cliff-dwelling to where The One was, he felt his gaze returned. "Welcome to the home, my brother," he thought, "welcome to the home."

The One, there with the People, remained in communion with his brother, the cliff-dweller. They felt each other and embraced. Yet even as He received the communion, The One's attention was drawn to the People who were once again stirring.

He sang them the Song of Peace, that they might rest a bit longer, that their spirits might be mended. Even as He sang the Song of Peace, the being of dark blue gazed upon Him. Their eyes met and as he heard the Song of Peace, the dark blue being stood. As he moved, it was as if he were liquid, bound by flesh, dark blue, deep dark blue.

He turned and began to walk, beginning his own journey in the Land Within, placing his feet upon the well-traveled path. It was patted down and soft to his feet. Cleared of all pebbles and debris, it was a smooth path. His journey wound this way and that way, around the trees and around the great giant statues of rocks piled upon each other, reaching upward and upward, and he kept walking.

It was as he walked around the bend that he came upon it — a great giant shell as if from the seas of old, as if from before the time of the sands. It was sitting up on a rise and grown around it was soft green moss. Within it was water. As if going home, he went to it. Stairs passed by the shell and continued upward toward a clearing amongst the rocks. When he looked closer, he saw an entryway nearly covered with hanging moss and vines. Yet it was there. He saw it.

He thought he would walk up those stairs if he could only find where they began. Stretching his neck upward to see, he followed the steps around and around the mound of rocks and on the opposite side of the shell he found the beginning of the stairs, carved right into the land itself. Water trickled a little here and there, and moss and ferns grew along the sides of the mound. He ate some of the fruit hanging from the vines and then began to walk slowly up the narrow steps that wound around the side of the mound. As he came around to stand above where he had been before, he recognized the spot and continued onward until he was just above the great shell which first had drawn him near. Looking into the pool in the shell, he saw golden fish swimming there.

As he bent down to look closer, he felt a hand upon his shoulder. It was a warm feeling. He turned to see another, just as he — deep dark blue in color. They stood together, looking into each other's eyes. Tears formed and fell down his cheeks. She whispered, "There are others." Even though he wondered who they were and where they were, he was at peace exactly as he was.

The breathing in and breathing out of this Earth had proven to him to be a grand journey and that which he had left behind was behind. He faced this way now, on this journey, and was filled with life.

She began to speak with him of the Land Within, of the peoples there, of those exactly as themselves, and of the rhythm of her lively day. Then she said, "Come, let me show you the gardens."

He followed down the steps and around and a little way upon the path. Then she turned and pulled aside hanging vines, exposing the entryway to the gardens.

There, every blossom that had ever existed in the breathing in and the breathing out did bloom, from the very smallest to the very largest. He saw, and as he saw he felt himself become the blossoms. It was as if they themselves beckoned him to come around and greet them and experience them, and before he knew what he was doing, that was exactly what he was doing.

He walked and caressed the blossoms, reaching up to those hanging from above. Some were large, very large, larger than his whole being! "I could," he thought, "if I could stand a little taller, I'd fit right into this blossom." He went to another and another, following their call.

On one side of the garden grew a shower of tiny blossoms flowing even to greet his feet at the very edge of the path. As he walked around them, it seemed they were everywhere, even where he might sit. Blossoms of every color surrounded him at each turn.

Then it caught his eye. A large pool of clear, light blue water. He knelt to look and saw that even in the water were blossoms, floating atop and within. Before he knew it, they too beckoned him. He dove into his home of homes, feeling it all around him, and then to the bottom where he walked amongst the blossoms there.

Blue essence they were. White essence they were. A little red essence they were. Sparkling, sparkling just like the ones from his home. His heart rejoiced as he caressed one here and another there.

He felt movement and turned. There she was beside him. They walked together at the very bottom of the water, filling themselves with the beauty of the blossoms there. Even though there was a small memory tugging at him, he turned away from it and said to her, "Here. We are here."

Her thoughts said to him, "Do you remember? But, do you remember?"

He said, "I see now. I am now. These blossoms are now. Here we are together, now."

Even though her mind had traveled into her memories and played there, she came forward to be with him, and they traveled into the caverns where the water carried them. There, once again, he saw the great shells growing, some small and some very large.

As he gazed upon them, one large white shell opened. He flowed toward it and laid himself within to rest. She saw and knew that, as she had, his being would rest for a time in the home of homes. Slowly the shell closed, and he did rest in the caverns, in the water, in the garden, in the Land Within.

She returned up through to the hanging gardens and then to the path to her own residing place, up the little steps carved into land. "Another has arrived," she thought, and wondered if there would be more. Even though there were many in the Land Within, there were few exactly as she, and she did enjoy being together with them. The others had beckoned her to come and join with all of them in the Land Within. She still hesitated, for she did so enjoy being with those the same as she.

The woman of the Council had known of the Land Within, yet this was the first time she had placed her own feet upon the land itself. She had always been above, observing the Earth Mother...and then...she couldn't quite remember what had happened. Walking along the path, she paused. Putting her hand to her head and pushing back her long hair, she thought, "What did happen...?"

She wondered how she had ended up on the sands with those people who had cared for her. "And The One...who was He? In all the observing they had done," she thought, "they had never seen Him here."

She sat for a moment, and upon the branch of a tree beside her came a bird. His red and yellow feathers shone bright against the green leaves. He looked at her and she laughed aloud and then as quickly, placed her hand over her mouth to cover it. She couldn't remember when she had last laughed as she just had. It felt unknown, strange.

She laughed again for the sheer pleasure of feeling it within her and for looking at that brightly colored bird and the way he was turning his head this way and that way, looking at her first with one eye and then the other. Then he turned his head upward and sang her a song. She could see his throat vibrating. She heard the song and the soft melody filled her.

Her wondering about what had happened seemed to pass by and then he flew to another tree and then another. She felt as if he were calling her to follow and she did, as a child would, amongst the trees. All red he was, with a back of yellow, and as he flew from tree to tree, she followed. When she did, he tipped his head upward and sang his song to her.

She continued to play with him until she came to a clearing, and even though she was following the little bird, the clearing drew her attention. In the clearing there were others!

There appeared to be a great hole in the land, and there were others sitting around upon the rocks, casually speaking with one another. "What is that hole there? It seems to go so deep. There's nothing in there," she thought, "nothing at all."

As she pushed aside the branches of one tree just a little so that she might enter the clearing, some of those who were gathered there saw her, and one woman went to her saying, "Welcome. We've been waiting for you." The woman took her hand and they walked together toward the others.

"She's here," the woman called out to the others.

They all looked up at her. She could feel their love. Women, all of them, with long, flowing hair, some red, some golden, some dark, some deep dark brown. Then she saw! Then she saw! On the shoulder of each robe was a golden emblem the same as hers! As she reached up to touch the one on her own robe, they smiled at her.

Including her, they were eight in all. They motioned her to come, and she and the one whose hand she still grasped tightly walked together. Before she knew it, they had gathered about her and then motioned again for her to follow.

She thought to herself, "I thought they were gathered here around this hole and that they were waiting here."

One heard her thoughts and said, "We thought you were coming through this entryway. Come along. We've much to show you."

She looked at the deep hole and wondered as she followed them, pausing only for a moment to turn and look about at the wonderful Land Within. She saw great structures, stones piled atop stones, land piled upon land, and caverns, deep caverns, and that great palace there. It felt to her as if she were in the dream of her dreams.

As she turned back to them, the little bird flew to her shoulder and then lit upon the finger of the woman who still held her hand. "You did find her, didn't you?" she said to him.

They brought her along the winding paths until again there was a clearing where she saw white vines twisted together one way and then another, and upon the vines were silken pillows the color of the sun. They motioned her toward them and she laid herself down.

They gave her a container of clear liquid to drink. It was so clear that she could see her fingers through it as she raised the container to her lips. She drank the liquid and it filled and nourished her. Then they placed food before her and they all ate together, and even as they were about her, she laid her head down upon those pillows and breathed a deep sigh. As she lay there, she felt...home.

The vines swayed slowly and gently, holding the pillows and her upon them, and she rested. Together they numbered eight.

In this manner the Land Within received its people.

And even as the breathing in occurred, the Land Within thrived, and the great Earth Mother did shake herself free.

CHAPTER TWENTY-TWO

There Was Once a Drop of Water

In the natural rhythm of the Land Within, there came the time of the Gathering, when all beings came together, partially for the purpose of union and partially for the purpose of gathering together those who had recently entered the Land Within, that they might be embraced and that, in the telling of the story of the Land Within, they might understand more deeply what it was that occurred about them — and beyond them.

At the top of the great structure, on the balcony of the palace, stood one being who placed to his lips a great shell. He blew into it and the sound resonated throughout the entire Land Within. Three times he blew into the great shell and three times the sound resonated throughout the Land Within.

Thus the Gathering began. There were those who had already begun to gather, even before the sounds were heard, for they knew it was the time of the Gathering. There were those who had just arrived and didn't even know such a thing as the Gathering existed. Those who were accustomed to this celebration went to those who were new and, speaking with them, brought them along.

It is this call that awakened those with The One. As they looked about at each other and then at Him, his smile filled them again. "Come, it is the time of the Gathering," he said. "Now you will see the others of whom I have been speaking, the others who also gather here."

Traveling throughout the Land Within was their joy, for around each corner of the path they were nourished by the sights and sounds and breaths of air. Even when they placed their feet upon the path, they felt strength flow into them. They felt it with each step and even as they walked, part of their very beings were awakened. They felt nourishment flow into them even at the sight of a blossom.

Soon they saw it. They had seen it once before and passed by. There it was, a grand golden field, and walking upon the steps carved right into the land, they followed Him as he stepped downward and downward and downward, into the great expanse. Even as they stepped downward, they saw beings on other stairways also carved right into the land.

The opening, like a great bowl, was so large that as they looked across they could barely see the features of the others, yet they did see them moving downward. The stairs led them to the bottom of the great bowl where they were standing on the edge of the golden field.

As they walked along the edge, they saw others walking along the edge and soon they all encircled the great, golden field. Those with The One looked around and saw the others, the ones He had sung about and told stories about. They were finally together. It was as if the breath of the Land Within breathed upon them freshness, newness of being. They felt it.

A young woman walked onto the field toward the center and stopped about midway. Then they all stopped circling and stood where they were.

The People with The One looked at Him and looked at the woman in the field and then, as they looked about them, they saw that some of the others were exactly as they. There, across the way, they saw the dark blue being and with him others exactly as he. Exactly as he!

They searched with their eyes for the woman. Yes, they saw her, the woman who had come to them with her long hair flowing and a golden emblem upon her robe. She saw them also, for she too had been searching. With her, they saw other beings exactly as she.

There were others they had ever seen before, some still with green glowing on them. They recognized that green glowing, for they had had it upon themselves for a time. They thought, "These beings must have just entered the Land Within." Still, the green glowing continued to emanate from those others.

There were those who were tall, very tall, interspersed amongst them all encircling the field, tall and filled with light. The People looked around and around and saw who else was there in the Land Within.

When everyone had settled within themselves, the young woman began to speak.

"We are the People.
We gather together
that you might know who we are.

"We are these in number.
This is our home.
This is your home.

"Long ago, here we did reside.
Here is our lifely vibration.
From within this great land
We have taken form,
and within form, this, then, is our home.

"Here then is every manner of form.
Here then is every manner of nourishment.

Here then is beauty.
Here then is the whole.
Here then is home.
Here then we gather together.

"This is your family.
We are your family.
See you, each one.
Then you would be..."

Even as she spoke the words, they looked about again and saw others sitting and they also sat, in the deep bowl, on the edge of the golden field. They felt the Land Within surround them.

Then there came another to stand in the field. It was the boy with the staff. They knew him well. He also spoke.

"There came the day," he said, "when I heard you calling me. Oh, I didn't know it was you calling me. But I felt the call and I gathered a few things together and left the village in which I lived. I began a journey.

"I began a journey," he repeated, looking about at them, "and on this journey, I met another who was also on a journey. We traveled together and felt light and filled with joy. Then we met another and another. It appeared we all had felt a calling and we really didn't know where we were going," his young voice said clearly, "but we were all traveling on a journey.

"One evening we gathered together, all of us. As we gathered together here in this field, my mind filled with those memories. We stood together then just as we are here, in a circle. In the center we built our campfire and there was one who came and sang the Song of the Journey. She sang it well and as we all listened, it felt as if she were singing us our own song.

Then another danced the dance, around and around, and we felt ourselves dancing, even as we watched him. I had never seen anything like it before," the boy said.

"Even then, when I looked around at those encircling the campfire, I could see that there were those who were not surprised and there were those who were as surprised as I was. At that time, I thought perhaps they were feeling like me, that this was brand new, and it felt...it felt wonderful!

"Then there came into the center of our circle a Great One. He stood there. He gave us bread and we ate together. He laughed a deep laugh and when he laughed a deep laugh, I felt as though I were laughing, myself. Never had I felt that before. And before I knew it, I was laughing too! And so were the others.

"Then we embraced each other and I found myself embracing people, people I had never known, and yet I felt as though I had known them forever.

"Then we lay down to rest and when I awakened, a great darkness was around. I thought someone had let the campfire go out. It was cold and dark."

The memory of it quivered in his voice. "I felt alone. I saw an ember and yes, I blew on it, placed sticks upon it and began to feel a little warm. The darkness lifted.

"But when it lifted, I truly was the only one there. And I want to know," he called out to them, "I want to know, is there anyone here who was there? Is there anyone here who was there with me?

"I don't know where they all went, but they went away, and yes, I did continue on my journey...but is there anyone here who was there?"

He stood there, the young man with the staff in his hand, and asked. He looked around, searching for one. Then from the other side of the circle, one being stepped forward. A man, a little hesitant at first.

He said, "I remember. I remember now! I remember!" And as if there were no center, no midway, no circle, he ran straight to the boy with the staff. "Yes," he said, standing in front of him. "Yes, I was there with you."

The boy looked at him for a moment and then recognized his face. He was the one who had gathered the sticks for the campfire. They grabbed each other's arms and then embraced and as they did, every being felt their embrace within themselves.

Words bubbled from the man. "Until this moment I had forgotten everything. I only knew I was here. I'm not even sure how I came to be here. But that campfire, I do remember that, and I do remember you!" They embraced each other again and stood drinking in the familiarity and knowingness of a time they had shared, similar, yet quite different from the Gathering they stood within. No one spoke; there was no hurry. After a time, they walked together to the edge of the circle and joined the others.

Then The One stood, and His great being came forward. He walked directly to the center of the golden field and called upon the boy with the staff. "Come."

The boy went to Him, carrying his staff. In the center, in the very center of the field, there was a little hole and the boy saw it and knew. He placed the staff there. And there it stood.

The One caressed the top of the boy's head and placed His great hand upon his shoulder. "You have done very well."

Then The One leaned back his head and laughed a deep laugh. The boy remembered, remembered his journey and touched his finger to the staff. It lighted a great light, emanating golden-white light. It resonated a sound.

Those around the circle clapped their hands together, each one saying, separately and together, "He has returned the staff!" Others watched, for it was new to them.

The Great One began to speak, and as He began, those around who had heard the story before leaned backward and placed themselves comfortably so that they might hear the story.

"There once was a drop of water," He began, "and as it dropped upon the Land Within, a sound was made that echoed throughout the Land. And as the sound echoed through the Land Within, the heralding of the light began. And then there was light in the Land Within and the light shone forth.

"As the light shone forth, beckoned were the plants and the trees, and growths of all kinds did spring forth in the Land Within. With the plants came the breathing — the breathing in and the breathing out, the breathing in and the breathing out.

"In the hand of one plant, there came to be a nest and from the nest came many flying beings and they filled the Land Within. From the flying beings came the song of songs, and melodies filled the Land Within.

"On the sounds of song came the beckoning. In the beckoning came the bringing to form of one being, and that one being is you. That one being is you.

"Come together. Come together." He motioned them to come to Him. "Come. For you have called yourselves together. You have called yourselves together. It is your own beckoning that you have heard. You have called yourself to return.

"It is your breath you have breathed."

Even as He spoke, they rose and first one and then another began walking to the center. Those who were seemingly new began to walk also, following the others.

As He stood there, He placed His great hand upon the glowing staff and he became The Lightbeing. The One was no more. The One was essence of light.

Each one walked to the center and, stepping into the light, became the light. Each one, stepping forward. Even those who were new, even those last ones who had followed The One stepped forward for they knew The One, they knew His love and they stepped into the center. And they too became the light.

It wasn't as if they were no more. It was as if they were much more, much more. They felt themselves and they felt the others. They were light, essence of light in the center.

Lastly, the child stepped forward. He saw the light and even as he stepped forward toward the center, the light seemed to gather together, closer and closer, closer and closer, until...until the light formed a large ball in the center.

Even as he walked closer, the ball seemed to condense, tighter and tighter, closer and closer, until, as he reached his little hand forward, the light was a tiny ball, so bright, so white, golden-white.

The child lifted the ball and placing it between his two little hands, he held it to himself, as if he were embracing it, for he did love the light. Soon, as he embraced the ball of light, *he* began to glow more and more, and more and more.

Finally, it was as if there were light embracing the light! And in the very center of the Land Within, there was union. The One was The One once again. One being. One light. One mind. One heart. Knowingness. Truth. Wisdom. One.

The One.

The One had called upon itself to gather together and even in the farthest reaches, every part heard and came.

Even from the very center of the Earth Mother, light filled her and then flowed outward, and from the top of her being, the light spilled forth and down and around, encircling her as she did spin.

The great Earth Mother, born of The One.

The great Earth Mother, born of The One.

The great Earth Mother, born of The One.

CHAPTER TWENTY-THREE

We Are from the Planet Lockspar

A message to all beings:

We are from the Lockspar planet beyond your calculations. Lockspar is a world beyond the galaxies you know. Until this occurrence, we had little cause for coming here, as our manners are presented differently. We have been watching changes occurring in several universes.

Our rapidity of form brings us beyond all other universes; thereby observation of changes is slow. These changes which have occurred in your planetary core have, for us, taken what you call millennia of millennia.

And now the change has occurred. Within the core of your planet, there has been condensing. You have called this "union." In the condensing there is produced quickening, quickening of this planet in the spinning. With the quickening, then, you enter our sphere of existence.

There comes to this planet another force from yet another galaxy. This has not been our concern until the present; any clashing of forces would directly affect us. We present ourselves to you to alert you that there comes another. Clashes appear to be imminent.

Lockspar derives direct causal of existence from the patterns formed through this quickening. As the quickening brings you to us, in time concept, we are prepared to participate, that the clashing would occur in a manner of least proportions for our continued existence. Thus, we present ourselves in this manner for your knowledge.

Aside from the effects on us, we have little cause for intercession or communication, as many galaxies, universes, exist. Yet this quickening has brought us here and thus we meet in another way than by observation.

Oh planet of light, prepare yourself for clashing of another coming to you! Awaken yourselves.

Then we would depart....

CHAPTER TWENTY-FOUR

It Had Been a Clashing of Old

There came forth a call, and within the core of the Earth Mother, The One — comprised of every being remaining upon the planet called Earth — received the call. Essence in light form, condensing and condensing, one being: The One.

It had been a clashing of old, and yet this time, the People gathered together in such force and solidity of form. The oncoming of the clash had been felt by many who had joined together to become The One.

Entering through the top of the Earth, it came flowing as thick liquid. Even as it slowly entered, there was a shudder within the Earth Mother. The thick liquid entered and flowed inward. Black it was, very black. And thick.

Slowly it came forward and the tiny hole through which it entered glowed, and the trickle became a little flowing, and the flowing became a river. Thick it was. Through the caverns it flowed.

Even as it flowed, the caverns opened wider. The walls seemed to dissolve with its flowing. Soon it entered the Land Within. Even at the first entry into the Land Within, they knew. Those of The One knew.

One being turned and saw. The People felt themselves think together, hear together, see together, be together. Taking form, one heartbeat together, one being — The One — turning to where the dark flowing entered the land.

It was nearly a choking feeling, the knowingness of it all. And yet, The One stepped forward to seek out where it was entering this land. Then He knew: the deep cavern.

There The One went, with great strides, a giant in His own land, and there He saw it. As it entered into the land, His land, the land of the People, it began to take form.

Even as it took form, it began to be in form, just like The One, and even as The One watched and felt, the thick black liquid flowed. Taking form and flowing, it began to fill the cavern. Alarm went through The One. Alarm!

Blessed are those who gather in the hearing
of this tale. Your strength, your wisdom,
your heart of hearts, your joy, your peace,
are felt in The One, for
You Are The One.
And so the battle begins.
We are ever present.

The entirety of the Land Within was alerted. Something was occurring there, something different, quite different, from the natural rhythm. All forms awakened to their fullest potential. The blossoms, the trees, the birds in the trees, the nests of the birds, the flowing waters, the tiny moss aside the brooks, the piles and piles of rock upon rock, and the sands, the Earth. Every part of the Land Within awakened to its fullest potential.

For there was entering — they could feel and know — the force of dissemination, dispersement of form, that none would gather. Dispersement. That even that which attracts like, like upon like, would be dispersed. The very essence of every life force in the Land Within felt the pulling. It was quite similar and yet different, so very different, from the expansion of their being. Nearly, nearly the feeling of pulling apart!

The consciousness of the Land Within thrived now upon The One, the unity of every being in one, one mind, one heart, one spirit. The one totality of every being remaining yet upon the planet called Earth Mother united together, forming one, one Lightbeing — The One.

The thick dark liquid came forward around The One, taking form as The One. Upward and upward it formed until it was as if The One were staring at The One. And yet it grew and grew and grew, larger than The One, larger, until it loomed over!

The One leaned back His head and from the very depths of His being, He released a laugh...deep laughter, the laughter so familiar, echoed through the Land Within.

The black form changed, changed once again. There, standing before The One, was a great, great serpent winding himself around The One. Thick, black, winding himself around and around until even His legs were bound together, winding upward and upward until The One was nearly choking. Thick darkness.

The glow of the Land Within changed ever so slightly to the glow of red. All the birds residing in the Land Within gathered together and in a rainbow of their own colors sang their songs. Tilting back their heads, their throats vibrated and they sang their songs.

The vibration of the sound echoed throughout the Land and the serpent unfurled. The One stood, breathing deeply. Joining in with the birds, He sang the Song of Praise for the song itself.

The serpent unfurled and again flowed like a thick black river. The One stepped toward it and reached to grasp it. His hand went through it. There was nothing to grasp! The blackness flowed and flowed through the very center of the Land Within.

With three long strides, The One was ahead of it, standing in its path. The thick dark liquid grew and grew, as if building upon itself, and there came toward The One a wall. It was thick and dark, a wall of growing darkness moving toward The One.

He stood His ground. There, holding His arms upward and outward, a deep sound came from within His being: "Noooooo!" He intoned deeply and loudly, "Noooooooooo!"

The thick black liquid that had formed into the wall continued! It came closer and closer to The One, and even as He stood His ground, the thick black wall covered Him.

It was as if he had been a small stick in the way. The blackness continued over Him and through the Land Within. It continued from one end to the other, a strong, dark, liquid river.

The light in the Land Within changed again to a deeper, deeper red. The One was as a stick. The grand structure of the grand being was held there as the blackness flowed over Him.

The light in the Land Within began to dim a little, and then a little more. Moment by moment, it dimmed and all the force of life within the Land felt itself pulling apart. The essence, creation, was pulling apart.

It was as if two forces lay upon each other: one force of union and light and another force of darkness and dissemination. As they lay upon each other, The One of Light let Himself flow and let the force of dissemination — just a little — enter His being.

He became as a river Himself. It was not quite as bright, yet still it was light, and He let Himself flow as the river. Soon, wherever the darkness flowed, under it all was a river of light, dim, yet a river of light! It flowed everywhere.

Together, the darkness and the light flowed as if in a race, quickly around, here and there in the Land Within. Wherever the dark serpent went, the light serpent went, winding together. Wherever the dark river went, the light river went, even to the waterfalls and down, darkness and light together.

Even as there came one tiny white blossom, in the center was dark black. First one and then the other; the essence of the blossom strained to be. The darkness strained to manifest darkness. The light strained to manifest light.

The Earth Mother, the great Earth Mother, began to tremble. The great Earth Mother began to shake, for the forces within, in the very center, in the very core, battled each other. The great Earth Mother began to roll about as if her spinning had changed a little.

From the very core of her being, from the battles of darkness and light, there came forth a flame. Upward it came through the caverns and outward, outward, outward until flames covered the entire Earth Mother. Hurtling, hurtling through the universe she did go, all aflame.

And even as the hurtling occurred, the battle continued.

There were those who observed. There were those who saw the hurtling.
There were those who saw the great Earth Mother change her course. There
were those who saw the hurtling fireball called the great Earth Mother.

Of all the galaxies together, there were those who watched. And they did, in
the galaxies and across the galaxies, form a sea, a sea of blue essence, that the
great fireball rushing toward them, upon entry into their universes might be
slowed, might be cooled; that the entry into their systems might be of a more
gentle nature than the flaming world coming toward them.

As the ball of fire entered the new domain, it entered the sea of blue essence
and slowed a little. The flames cooled a little. Still moving, it continued
through the blue sea.

Those who observed saw the slowing. Those who observed saw the flames
begin to diminish.

From an opening at the top of the planet called Earth Mother there came
forth a liquid, flowing as a river. Dark it was, flowing outward and outward.

As it flowed outward, it formed a ball, a ball of darkness, and it grew and grew and
grew, until it was nearly the same size as the planet called the Earth Mother. It was as
if there were two planets, one atop the other: one of darkness and one of light.

Then the spinning began, each one spinning in the opposite manner, and as
the spinning began, the two planets began to part, spinning away from each
other. There formed then, two planets: one of darkness and one of light.

The Planet of Light did spin, and the golden-white light shone its beauty in
the new domain.

The two found their places in the new domain.

The great Earth Mother breathed her breath outward once again.

*Even in this grand, grand universe of universes of yet more universes, there
are those of us who observe and guide. And even in the guiding, there is wonder,
for each being in this grand universe vibrates according to the consciousness of its
own self, even unto each individual.*

*And when one, through action, changes a course, it would be a direct result
of following that consciousness. Not one consciousness is right or wrong. Each
exists.*

*Therefore, this assistance has been given through the consciousness of that
universe in which the new Earth Mother does now reside. And yet, there are
many more universes upon universes.*

PART III

The Story
of the People

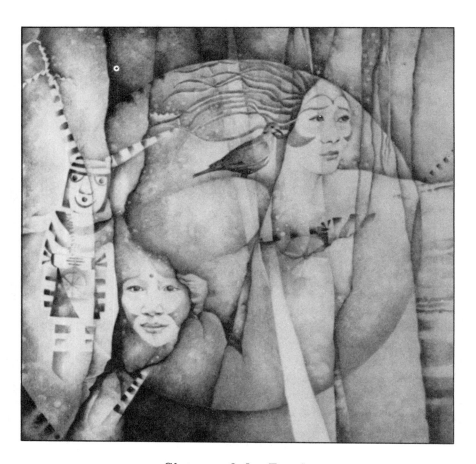

Sisters of the Earth

"As the People gathered about, excitement grew within their limbs. Today the Old One will come down from the mountain and speak with them. He is the One who came from within the great Earth Mother."

CHAPTER TWENTY-FIVE

The Old One Did Hear the Sound of the Shell

The Story of the People has no beginning and no end. It is simply the tale of those beings residing within the great Earth Mother, the tale of the great Earth Mother breathing in and breathing out, the tale of the relations between the People and the Earth Mother.

The Preparation

It was a day of great celebration and preparation, for upon the rising of the great Moon Mother, there would be the speaking of the tale, the Story of the People.

As the People gathered about, excitement grew within their limbs. Today the Old One would come down from the mountain and speak with them. He was the One who came from within the great Earth Mother.

There were only a few who had heard this tale three times before. The others waited, knowing that their beloved Old One would soon be amongst them.

Upon rising they gathered together and, in their usual way, formed a circle while the children played in the center. They numbered thirty as they began singing the Song of Praise of this day: celebration of their being, celebration of the rhythm of their being, celebration of the day of preparation, for in the evening would be the telling of the tale.

Glowing with joy, they looked across at each other and then at the little children who played and scampered about, hugging the legs of one, running to another and hugging the legs of another, laughing all the while. They sang the Song of Praise for the Children.

After the morning gathering, little groups began the preparations. Three Warriors silently carried gourds of colored sands to the clearing at the base of the mountain. There, upon their Holy Grounds, they began to paint upon the Earth Mother their truth. They painted first a circle and then within, two lines crossing each other; then rays coming outward from the great circle.

Within one of the four sections in the circle, they painted a wheel as if it were spinning, spinning. In another section they painted a large, round black ball. In another section they painted fire, and in the fourth section they painted lines, wavy lines.

While they painted with the colored sands, they sang a song. It was rhythmic and yet sweet and light. When they were finished, they saw what they had done and then quietly, ever so quietly, they departed.

Then came one Warrior carrying great armloads of sticks, carefully walking to the center of the circle and placing the sticks there in preparation for the lighting of the fire, which designated the beginning of the telling of the tale. When he was finished piling the sticks, he quietly left.

When all the preparations had been made, including baskets of fruit and urns of water, they then refrained from going there so that the grounds might rest and be.

Amongst themselves, they allowed the joy to build as they continued in the celebration of the day. One woman walked from her home across to another's and in her hands she bore her favorite article from her home. This she brought as a gift to the other and the other did receive.

One woman carried with her a great blue stone. It had resided in the very center of her home, and in praise of this day she lifted it with her two hands and carried it across to her friend.

She sang the Song of Praise of Giving and presented to her friend the blue stone. Her friend sang the Song of Receiving and of the beauty of the gift which she received. Together they bore the blue stone to the center of her friend's home and placed it there to reside.

In this manner, the People celebrated.

There was preparation of a great meal and then joining together, dipping their fingers into the paste and placing their fingers upon the lips of another, feeding each other until they were filled. Even the little children celebrated in this manner, laughing and laughing until they were nearly entirely covered with food.

Then they all returned to their own homes and rested quietly, each home carrying the gift given from another.

The Beginning: The First Day

At the time of the changing of the light of day to the light of night, a deep, resonant sound was made. One being, standing, heralded the arrival of the light of night, for he felt the beginning of the Old One. He sounded the sound, breathing his breath through the great shell.

They heard and rose quietly from their resting places and silently went to sit in that place which had been prepared for the telling of the tale.

The Old One heard the sound of the shell. Three times he heard the sound, even as he was stepping down the mountain. Several times as a young man, he had traveled to the top of this great mountain and received visions. Now he bore the name of the Old One, and he lived alone. In peace he lived. In silence he lived.

Yet on this day he spoke aloud to the Great One. "Oh Great One, today we shall share again our tale. Will you come before these people?" He thought of his beloved people and of all that had occurred thus far in his lifely vibration.

Many things the Great One had done with him, many visions had been given. He shook his head and laughed at himself a little, gathered his satchel and staff together and began his journey down the mountain.

He came to the place of the dwelling of another Old One. The dwelling was closed, for he alone was the only Old One remaining. He reached upward and asked that the spirits of the Old Ones be with him, that they all be telling this tale.

He traveled downward and soon reached the bottom of the mountain just as the light of day released to the light of night.

He stood upon the rise. As they saw him, their hearts flooded with joy. Light emanated from his being. They saw him and they saw his light. Standing in the circle, they sang the Song of Praise of his appearance.

The Old One watched the young man whose arms had borne the sticks step into the center, light the fire and return to the circle. In the flickering light could be seen the faces of the People. "My people," he thought, "my people."

He began telling the story, speaking of his visions and of the Great One calling to him. Even as he spoke, he sang the Song of Praise of the Visions, and those sitting about reveled in the hearing. Those few who had heard before breathed in the words, for they knew it was the tale of themselves and of their heritage.

Those who had not heard before leaned forward as if they might grasp the next word, even as it came from the Ancient One's lips, so ready were they to hear the tale. The children too sat quietly and listened.

The flowing of the words did weave amongst them peace. The flowing of the words did weave amongst them serenity. The flowing of the words did weave amongst them union.

And he continued on and on....

"There came the day, oh People," he said, "when, yes, we entered this great Earth Mother, and there were none other of the People except those of us who entered within. Into the bowels of her we traveled, and there, upon seven days of journey, we came upon a chamber. In the chamber we each found a place in which to rest and be.

"We began a long rest, a long sleep. And even as we laid ourselves down, we looked at each other, and we saw who we were. Then we did sleep."

He looked deep into their eyes as he spoke, uniting with their innocence, filling them with love. "The others did sleep," he continued, "and yet my sleep was restless. Great visions the Great One gave to me. Once again, visions of this Earth Mother breathing inward and outward. And then, even while the others slept, I felt rumbling under my feet. Rumbling so great I could not stand! I stayed in my resting place.

"Even as the sleep began to overtake me, I saw part of the chamber falling upon itself. Crashing rocks. Even though I wished to rise and help the People to see if you were still alive, still breathing the breath, the sleep did pull me and pull me and pull me. And there I did lie."

He paused, his gaze caressing the little ones resting their heads upon their mothers' laps. "The number of years it would take a child to become an Old One, we lay in slumber.

"Then there came a stirring in my limbs and I began to awaken. Darkness, there was darkness. I sat up and felt the flowing of life throughout my limbs and being. And as if from the beginning of a tunnel far away, there spilled forth a little light into the chamber. It were as if the Great One were giving me a vision again, and yet I could see.

"And I did see, oh People, I did see great rocks, tumbled this way and that way in the cavern. And I thought of you, oh People, and I looked about and looked about.

"At first, I thought there were none of you left. As I stood and began to walk about, I saw that the rubble of the rocks had but hidden you all from my sight. There you were, stirring, stirring, but three; all but three did awaken.

Tears already spilled down the cheeks of those few who had heard the story before. "Three. Our three treasures remained asleep. The Great One called the Father of our People remained asleep. The Great One called the Mother of our People remained asleep. And the child did remain asleep.

"The light beckoned us. We began to walk slowly, slowly, a journey toward the light. It was as if we were walking in the cracking of the Earth Mother. 'Twas not really a path upon which we walked.

"With difficulty, we climbed this way and that way, ways unfamiliar to us, for the paths upon the Earth Mother had always been smooth and well-worn. Here were jagged edges. And even as we walked, slashes came here and there upon our legs and our feet. Many times, oh People, we did sit and rest.

"The journey was long. The journey, dear ones, was difficult on many. Even as we reached midway, but one-half the number still remained.

"Even though we sang the Song of Praise of Life Force within our being, we became weak. Weak. Each day, even though we took barely twenty steps and rested, there came the day when we could feel the light-scented breath upon us. And we breathed, breathed life into our limbs.

"Then our journey from within to without nearly completed, we gathered together those few. Six we were, only six in number. And we viewed each other and rested together, barely able to sing the Songs of Praise.

"And there appeared before us a Great One. Even though in our weakness we could barely turn to see, we did see. As if in a vision, He appeared before us, and in His great hand, He did offer to us berries. We took them and pressed them to our lips. Even as we pressed them to our lips, He was gone.

"Then, dear ones, we felt a little strength flow within us, and we continued toward the light. Each of us pushed each other out of the great crack and crevice and stepped forward into the light.

"There, dear ones, was the great Earth Mother. It was as if she had been divided in half, a line drawn. One side of the line were the trees, the trees. Even as we viewed them, we felt strength returning, and the waters.

"And on the other side of the line was but sand. We saw sand, nothing but sand.

"We were weak, and the strength of the trees beckoned us. We took little steps, each helping the other, and we came upon the water, as if a very soft waterfall. The spray coming from the waterfall fell upon us.

"And there we did lie, dipping our hands into the water and placing them to our mouths, sucking on our fingers. We did, dear ones, for three days.

"Then the strength began to return to our limbs, to our beings. Even though our hearts ached, we felt the strength return. And when we could rise, we stood under the waterfall together, six in number. We allowed the waterfall to cleanse our beings. Flowing about us, cleansing our wounds. Our flesh felt union with the water and it replenished us.

"On the side of the banks we found the leaves of bushes and we bound them around our wounds and on our feet. This we did for the next three days.

"There were tiny berries along the bushes and these we fed to each other. Thus began our tradition of eating, that we would feed each other until we were all full. Only a few berries we ate initially.

"Then, on the fourth day, we ventured forward a little, for the leaves had bound and healed our wounds, and there we found trees with fruit, great fruit. We prepared a feast for ourselves and sang the Song of Praise of the trees and the fruit.

"And this was the beginning. This, then, was how we gathered together. Slowly, gently, with each other, we did care, care for each other's wounds and feed each other. We stayed within that place for a time, building the rhythm of our daily vibration.

"And yet, it was the time for the healing of our hearts, for we still ached for the others. So we traveled a little until, dear ones, we came to this very spot, to this clearing, to this field, and here we began.

"At first we began to walk, even in a circle, the six of us. And then, as if in a spiral we walked around and around until we were walking in a grand circle. It was as if the spirits of all the others walked with us. We felt them all, dear ones, walking with us, together. And we sang the Song of Praise of Our People. And we sang the Song of Praise of Our Unions.

"Therein we walked, around and around, together. And there was one amongst us of the six, a woman, who stepped into the center and she sang a Song of Praise of the Aching Heart. And even as she sang, the notes and the words and the sounds did swell our hearts, and we did weep together. We did weep together, and even the spirits of the Old Ones did weep with us.

"Then she sang the Song of Praise of who we are, the People, and the Song of Praise of this Earth Mother upon which we stood. And we felt within us, and even in the Earth Mother, even the heart of the Earth Mother was the aching. And we did sing the song to her.

"And our numbers grew. Yes, we did bear children amongst ourselves and our numbers grew. This, dear ones, was a new beginning, was our new beginning, was your new beginning."

Into the circle the Old One walked and he began to dance the dance of the People. And even as he danced the dance, they felt it flow within themselves and they began to dance also. Even the ones who had not seen the Ancient One before felt the rhythm of the dance.

There was one child who came forward into the circle. Laughing, laughing she was as she came to him. He gathered her in his hands and raised her upward, himself laughing. He placed her feet upon his and slowly and gently he began to dance. Soon they danced together, one being dancing.

In this manner, then, the Old One did teach the dance of old, the Dance of the Ancient One, Father of the Father, of the Father of the Fathers. For had he not seen that Old One teach the little ones even before they entered the great Earth Mother so long ago?

He spoke with them the tale of their ancestors before the entering of the great Earth Mother. They sat around the fire, and closer and closer they came. He spoke the words that the Father of the Father, of the Father of the Fathers did speak, teaching them their heritage.

He spoke the songs and the stories of the Ancient One of the Mother of the Mothers, of the Mother of the Mothers, teaching them songs of their beings so that they might know the heritage of themselves.

As he spoke, they became enriched. They felt themselves filling and filling with who they were. He knew that He would be with them for three days, and on the fullness of their great Moon Mother, then he would speak of her story also, black that she was, glistening, glistening in their sky.

He bid them rest about the campfire and he did sit, for the Old One had rested long enough, and he was with them as they rested on the completion of the first day.

Never fear for your story. You are the brave ones. You are the ones who have returned. Yes, dear ones. Think you have returned for naught? Never it'd be. Never would it be.

CHAPTER TWENTY-SIX

There Would Be Sent One Being

The planet called Earth then resided in the new domain, first cooling for thirty of your Earth years. Then for the period of five Earth years was the condensing, and the Earth then became a little smaller. From the heart of the Great Earth Mother came a sigh, as if a sigh of relief, for here in this new domain she did reside.

Then there came a period of rejuvenation, and expressions of life forms began. A tiny tree began here and a little bush there. The Earth Mother nourished herself. This then continued for thirty years. Yet in the place whence the new black moon had emerged, there remained but sands.

In the time of Lockspar, the rejuvenation of the new planet within their domain occurred in one thousand years. Such was the difference in the times of the two planets, each at different ends of the universe. During this time, the beings of Lockspar removed the last layer of blue which had protected their universe from the entry and moving about of the new planet and her black moon.

In the breathing out and breathing in of the great pulse-beat of the universe and the Earth Mother therein, there had been upon the Earth darkness and light, darkness and light.

Through the time of cooling and through the time of condensing and through the time of nourishing, there then came a time of new beginning, and the life force within the Earth Mother took form, and then there was the breathing out once again.

Though this time was long, the planet of Lockspar and the beings thereon felt the effects, for the entry of two new planets within their domain caused change. It changed their manner of vibrating. It changed their manner of life force.

Even as the planet Lockspar, the great Earth Mother and the black moon resided within the same domain, those amongst the other planets of this domain observed. Of those beings who traveled about this universe, not one traveled to the new planet or her black moon.

Even in the last exploration, upon returning to their home universe there were those who traversed around the Earth Mother so that they might view closer this brand new planet and her black moon.

In this most recent turning around, there were registered sophisticated patterns of form. It appeared that the most sophisticated of beings were once again upon the great planet called Earth. There was recorded movement there about the Earth, a new form. There had been something there.

Those observers felt a feeling deep within their beings. It was new. What was this feeling? Something resonated within them. It was new. However, upon their communications within their universe, they did say, "The Earthlings have returned! The Earthlings have returned! The Earthlings...have returned."

The message resounded throughout the universe of the new domain, and even amongst those who least expected it, there was a feeling within. There were some on the most distant planet of Lockspar who also felt a change within their beings and recognized the familiarity of the feeling: the Earthlings had returned; the feeling was joy.

For it was they, of them all, who had taken it upon themselves to become part of the destiny of the great Earth Mother and her new black moon, and they who had seen possibilities of her entering their domain and the possibilities of the effects therein.

They had gone to those people of the Earth and stated that they would assist in this great change. Even though the change upon the Earth Mother would seemingly be but a moment, yet for Lockspar it was nearly as long as the history of themselves. And now here the words came to them: The Earthlings had returned!

For the Earthlings and they, the beings of Lockspar, there was similarity of heritage — similarities in essence of being, similarities in the flowings of life force, similarities in the manner of creation and similarities in the manner of the heart.

It was decided upon the planet of Lockspar that there would then be sent one being, and that being would enter upon the planet called Earth and view the Earthlings and their manner of being, and to *directly communicate*, so that the similarities might be shared amongst the two planets of the new domain, each on the farthest end of this universe. The great Earth Mother and her black moon and the silver planet called Lockspar.

Then upon this day, the being of Lockspar took form upon the planet called Earth and viewed the Gathering of the People, the Earthlings.

The Second Day

As they awakened into the smiling eyes of their Ancient One, he began. "My people, this then be the second day of the telling of our story. And yes, I am the Old One of you all. This heart beats strongly and love emanates from it to you and holds you, as if this Old One were holding you as a child in his arms, cradling you, whispering in your ear, singing the songs to you softly, presenting to you the gifts of the visions and the heritage of your very own self.

"These eyes do see you clearly. They see you as you and as your fathers' fathers' father and as your mothers' mothers' mother and as the children before you, and as the children before they and as the children before they that bore the mothers' mothers' mother — these eyes do see this when they view you.

"For this Old One knows you," he continued, "and all of those of your heritage. And you ask, 'How could he know? How could he know the Old Ones? Even in all his years,' you think, 'he has not been around those Old Ones.' And yet I say to you, I am those Old Ones. Here, this day, you hear the Teaching of the People.

"For there came the day amongst us in the gatherings when the Old One turned from you and began the journey to the mountain. And even as we of the Old Ones have turned from you, we are with you ever, ever present.

"This you do know, for have we not been with you and returned to you, spoken with you, told you the stories of your own selves, told you the stories of others that you might know your heritage?

"And on this day, are we not here? Yes. And even though you know me as the Old One, even though amongst you long ago I was the great Warrior receiving the visions from the Great One and carrying them you, yes, I am that one and I am more. This day, then, is the Speaking of the Teaching. For in this new Earth Mother, with the new moon of black darkness glistening in the sky, the teachings change.

"You believe that this is the Earth Mother upon which you resided in your heritage? Two other Ancient Ones there are, two other Ancient Ones in the mountains, those of us who entered within the great Earth Mother and then came out again.

"Three are all there are of us, and we say to you: This Earth Mother upon which you reside is a new mother to you. And upon this new mother then, we spill forth these teachings that you might be resonating, for there is change amongst us. In your heritage, there was a time when there was marriage of a young man and a young woman and amongst the People there were celebrations. Therein there was the Dancing of the Dance and the Singing of the Songs.

"Then would be the time of the journey, then would be the time of the dreams, would be the time of the visions, would be the time of the great Warrior. And then, in our heritage, my dear ones, then would be the time for the Old One to go to the mountain, as I have done.

"In this day, I say to you, there is change. For from this day forward, you will not wait until you are the Old One to be at the mountain. This day, this mountain receives you. And you say, 'But yes, we must be an Old One to be so wise, to receive the visions of the mountain, to hear the stories and the singing of the Wind Spirit. We must be an Old One.'

"And this day we say you are the Old One. For the Old One, my dear ones, has very little to do with the numbers of years you have placed your feet upon this planet.

"My dear ones, you are *born* to be the Old Ones. Even with your first breath you are the Old One!" He paused a moment, searching their faces, knowing they needed more, more words, more time. And he continued. "Then we say to you, that you might know: When I turned from you to begin the journey on the mountain, I then began my journey to *become* the mountain, to become the Old One. You see? There was change within my being, and even though you viewed me as the Old One, I was still becoming the Old One.

"Upon this great mountain I began the journey, placing one foot and then another and then another upon the great path. When I came upon the first gathering place, therein I sang the Song of Praise of that place that it might open and receive me. He paused again, asking, "Why do we tell you this story this day? That at the instant you are called within your being, you might begin and you will know what to do! Yes!"

His words gently summoned their strength. "Then in the singing of the Song of Praise, the first gathering place was revealed to me as the branches of the trees unfolded. And there was presented a place of sitting. It was the moss of the mountains so close to the Earth, breathing. In the center of the moss of the mountains, there was a golden seat, and there I brought this body to sit. And sitting there, as soon as I breathed a deep breath, the branches on the trees did close about me.

"And you think, 'How long did he be there?' You think, 'How many moons?' This I do not know. For upon sitting there, the moons and the timing and the turning and the changing all went away from me, and there I did sit.

"Surrounding me, came the Ancient Ones and they spoke with me. I viewed them. Some there I recognized with what I thought were my eyes, yet I had brought this body to sit, and as I looked, there it was, sitting! And as this body was sitting, there I was walking about them, as if I were the Spirit of the Ancient One, yet I could still see this body sitting there. Amongst them I walked and they spoke with me. Together we journeyed within, into the cavern behind the sitting place. And there we saw together urns, vials of oils. There we saw together hides. There we saw together barks of the trees. There we saw together writing. There we saw together balls of light. There we saw together a golden staff. There we saw together those drawings which we have spoken of together. All this we saw together. And the Ancient Ones said to me, 'This is your heritage also.' And there I saw the vials and the drawings.

"And then the Ancient Ones began to swirl and swirl about as if a great wind spirit had come amongst them, as if they were the clouds in the sky. They swirled about me, even as I stood there. And as they swirled about, dear ones, they entered this being. It was as if the spirit within this body had been filled with the clouds of the Ancient Ones.

"And the One Voice of the Ancient Ones did speak with me: 'You are with us now. And we are with you.'

"Twice more they showed me: swirling, they came out from my spirit and formed before me, the Ancient Ones. Then as clouds again, they swirled together and entered this being. Upon the third time, they said, 'Then the sealing of this door.'

"Then, dear ones, this spirit did enter the sitting body. It felt this body. It filled this heart. It filled these eyes. Then, dear ones, I stood and the branches parted and I stepped forward. And yes, then I was the Ancient Ones. You see?"

His great love joined their wonder as he continued. "Yet the journey had just begun for this one before you. I continued up the mountain to the top.

"Why do I say this to you? So that when you journey the mountain and you sing the Song of Praise and the branches open and you see the golden seat and you sit there, then you would know. Yes. Yes! This is your heritage. Yes.

"And you think, 'When?' And some of you think, 'No, I will not.' And yet, each one will do this. We tell you this for your heart, for the yearning in your heart, for the day when you will be the Ancient One. And yet, you are that one now. We speak this teaching so that then, upon your journey, you will know it to be true.

"Then we continued to the top of the mountain. We say this, dear ones: It was a joy for this one to discover strength of the Ancient Ones. For even though these feet began to walk upon the path, when this mind thought of the top of the mountain, next, we appeared there! This spirit and this body! Yes! The Ancient Ones together as one.

"When we climbed to the top of the mountain, sometimes these feet walked and sometimes they did not. I then remembered the children, for it was as play.

"And this we say to you dear ones: This is your heritage. This is your heritage."

And even as he spoke with them, they felt within themselves strength. And even as he spoke of his heart of hearts, they felt within themselves the love of the universe. And even as he spoke with them of the seeing, they began, here and there, to have visions, little familiar flickerings. They knew them from the time of dreaming.

Their Ancient One spoke with them of the newness of his being. Never before had they heard these words. Even as he said the words himself, never before had the People received these teachings.

They felt alive! They were ready. They had wanted these teachings. They hadn't known what teachings they were, but now here they were, presented to them.

Not one wondered why at this time, out of any other time, would be the revealing of the teachings of the Ancient Ones. Not one wondered. They all leaned forward so that they might hear. They all leaned forward so that they might bask in the glow of their Ancient One.

In this teaching, He spoke with them and it was nearly the end of the second day as they gathered about to sing the Song of Praise of the Teaching, to sing the Song of Praise of the Ancient Ones, to sing the Song of Praise of who they were.

Even as they gathered then, the one being who was viewing them all did prepare to step forward, the one being from that distant planet called Lockspar.

Even as they were viewing their Ancient One, a silver, silver essence formed beside the Ancient One. Glowing in silver until another being took form beside the Ancient One! The Ancient One remained sitting, quiet.

They wanted to lean forward, and yet they pulled back a little. Who was this being? Was this their Ancient One playing with them? Demonstrating the teaching for them?

Yet this being did take form — silver, glowing. He stood there looking at them and then he spoke.

"We are from there." He pointed. "Beyond the beyond, we reside. We have been observing your planet called Earth. We have seen you here. Joy fills our beings."

He continued in his monotone voice, "We registered joy amongst ourselves. Even though we speak a different language from yours, we have come here to your home to speak as well as we are able. For in all of this universe, you and we are brothers. This planet, your home of Earth, has been beyond our concerns; but now we are in a direct line.

"Even though we appear to be different, we are quite similar. If you would have us amongst you, then you would see our similarities.

"This, then, be the reason we come here this day. We are brothers. We are the same.

"This Ancient One is our Ancient One. This form of body-being is different from the form of body-being of our Ancient One. Yet, this is our Ancient One, as he is yours.

"The Ancient Ones live beyond the top of this mountain, beyond the top of your home planet called Earth, beyond the spinning black moon above, beyond this universe, beyond this domain they do reside.

"We will be amongst you for several of your days. We are brothers. We are the same. You will see this. We see this."

As quickly as he had appeared, then he was gone. The People looked at the place where he had stood, and then from there to their Ancient One; to the place and to the Ancient One, back and forth they looked.

Their Ancient One continued to sit, to be.

And what did the People do? They sang the Song of Praise for their heart of hearts. They sang the Song of Praise for the visions. They sang the Song of Praise for their Ancient One. And they sang the Song of Praise for the being who called them brother.

This then did occur on the second day of the three days with the Ancient One of the mountain.

Blessed be those beings who receive the telling of this tale.

CHAPTER TWENTY-SEVEN

And They Began to Teach the Children

The black moon had also cooled. Yet within its core remained a ball of fire, a furnace. As it spun, the outer layers cooled and the life force retreated to the core. As it retreated, behind it came solidification and the black moon became hard and solid with the life force within its core.

Glistening as it spun, its beauty shone for all to see. There were those upon Lockspar who observed the black moon as they had observed the solidifying of other planets whose paths and spinning had become quite predictable, and it was for this reason that they breathed a breath of relief when they observed the solidifying of the black moon.

Those of Lockspar had seen the birthing of the black moon. They had seen the Earth Mother in its metamorphosis, giving the last shudder of birth. Those forces which were different from her natural state of being had followed the darkness from within her to without and into the forming of the new black planet. The beings of Lockspar saw and felt, even unto their own core.

And now a new time had begun. One of them was upon the Earth Mother and indeed was speaking with the Earthlings! Even in the records, they began anew.

When their representative spoke with the Earthlings, all the beings of Lockspar experienced the speaking, for with them, where one was they all were. They felt the ripple flow through the Earthlings and they felt within themselves rejoicing.

Of all the great planets within their systems, there were few whose dwellers could receive the vibrations of their beings and who were capable of hearing even what would be spoken. With the increase of the spinning and the condensing of the Earth Mother, the change within her vibration was exactly the correct amount. Now they could begin communication. Yes, there was rejoicing.

The Beginning of the Third Day

At the beginning of the third day of the speaking with their Ancient One, the People prepared themselves for the hearing of the Truths. Standing in the soft spray of the waterfall, they cleansed their beings and breathed in the sweet scent of flowers. Placing the tiny white blossoms in their hair, they gathered the most beautiful blossoms for their Ancient One.

He gazed upon them. His love beckoned them. They came and placed the sweet white blossoms in his hair. He received their gift of love, their gift of purity. As they stood near him, nourishment flowed from him into them and like hungry children, they settled closely around as he began to speak.

"Then, dear ones," his voice enveloped them, "upon this day, the third day, we will speak those words which have not been spoken before: the journey to the top of the mountain.

"Why do we speak these words with you?" He looked into their upturned faces. "It is a new time, a new beginning. After these days, the Ancient Ones will no longer come amongst you. This is your beginning. This is your day of days. Now.

"Dear ones: You are the Old Ones. You are the Ancient Ones." His words entered and filled them. His great arm motioned upward. "This mountain is yours. Place your feet upon the path, that path you have reserved for the Old Ones, that path those before you and those before you and those before you have been reserving for the Ancient Ones. Now you walk these paths.

"Why would it be I," he pointed to himself, "even as a young boy, who walked the path to the top of the mountain? Why, of all the others, would it be I?" Leaning forward he whispered, "You say 'Because the father of my father's father was the Ancient One also'? And do you not know that the father of the fathers' father was father of us all? What then is the difference between you and me? And yet, I did walk that path in my youth to the top of the mountain.

"There, did a Great One come to me? Yes. I carried the vision down to you, that you might know. Yes, the stories have been told again and again and you know this occurred.

"This day, these words I do say: It is *your* path upon that mountain. The path for *your* feet, for there is no difference between you and me. We are the same. It is a new beginning."

They heard his words and felt them moving within, felt the truths filling them, and even beyond their thinking, they knew.

"From this day then, you are the Ancient Ones coming amongst yourselves. In your heart of hearts, you know even beyond these teachings. Within yourselves, you feel the truths and you will journey beyond the beyond."

Then he continued the telling of his own journey. "As I walked without effort upward, there it was — the top of the mountain. And there I stood, remembering the visions that had come to me, remembering the words, remembering the Great One. There, with all of Them within me, I did be, and the wind spirit blew about and within me and breathed my breath. There I sat for three days.

"In the sitting, there was no difference between the top of the mountain and me. Where my being ended and the mountain began drifted from my knowingness and I became the mountain. Therein the trees grew upon me, and the birds came and walked upon me." His loving eyes turned upward. "Therein I did be and feel my being growing and growing and growing until I was the entirety of the mountain and the mountain the entirety of me, and then even more until I became this great Mother Earth and this great planet became me. And I felt you walking upon me. I felt you singing your Songs of Praise. I felt your laughter. I felt the depths of this great Earth Mother and I became the depths and they became me.

"And you say, 'What kind of story is this? How can this be?' " His smile caressed them. "Place your feet upon your mountain and begin, for no longer will we come amongst you and tell these tales. No longer will you gaze upon a being separate from yourself and feel the nourishment flowing."

He raised his great body and stood before them. "For this is the new day! This is the day of days wherein *you* are the Ancient Ones." He pointed at each one as he spoke. "You walk the path upon the mountain. You become the mountain, for you are the People." He outstretched his arms, "For this purpose, the People have gathered upon this great Earth Mother, and this day of days begins the fulfillment of that purpose!" The words echoed, repeating themselves again and again.

"There has been one other who has come amongst you, even on the second day, and has spoken of his home afar. Know this to be true: From the top of the mountain, you can travel to his home. You can be anywhere! You can be anything! For then you, dear ones, are the Ancient One. Yes, that being has spoken that you are brothers. It is true, this you are and more, and much more.

He Speaks of Much More

"There was once a People who resided in the center of this great planet. They gathered their essence into being and formed and lived within the Earth Mother.

"There then came the time of the breathing of the Earth Mother. She breathed outward and inward. Upon one of her breaths, she bore the People outward to reside upon her where before they had resided within. They thrived and grew in number and honored the Earth Mother which had borne them outward.

"Then came the breath again, and those who were living without, upon the Earth, were breathed within so that they might remember whence they came. The People resided within once again.

"There came again the time of the breathing out, and there were those within who clung to the Earth Mother, beseeching, 'Let us remain here, for within you we are who we are. Without, we forget who you are and who we are.'

"The breath allowed them to stay and still carried others without. Then, for the first time, there were People living within and without.

" 'Twas the end of the breath of the Earth Mother for a very long time, dear ones. Then again came the time that she breathed her breath, and those People who lived without clung that they might remain there. They had forgotten about the breathing within. The breath allowed them to remain, and only a few returned within. Those who did return saw and felt and remembered who they were.

"Again the breathing ceased, dear ones, for a long time. Then again it began. There were those who were living within who clung to the within lest they be without and forget once again who they were.

"And the breath allowed them to be, and only a few were breathed outward. They placed their feet upon the Earth and walked amongst the People. While they traveled, they spoke amongst themselves of what had occurred with the People and how they had forgotten who they were, how they had forgotten the grandness of their beings.

"Then, to be with themselves, they walked on the path to the top of the mountain. Thus began the truth: They walked to the midway of the mountain and resided. There they asked the Earth Mother to breathe the breath of knowingness upon them, lest they forget who they were, lest they forget their grandness.

"The Great Ones visited upon them within and without, and they rejoiced in communion.

"This then was the forming of the truth of that residing place of which we have spoken — your residing place.

"Those few People, glowing, filled with light, joy upon their faces, hearts filled with love, then walked back down the mountain and amongst the others. The others saw them and like a magnet drawing to itself the People drew the others to them, and they gathered around. Some of the People they placed upon thrones to be their kings. Others they placed above them so that they could bow before them, the Queen, the Great Mother of themselves.

"Others followed as if following a Great One, and wherever he went, they went, until there was soon a little gathering of a family about that One. Again and again it happened and small gatherings began. Those who had gathered around the Lighted Ones began to awaken a little and a little more, and there was great rejoicing.

"Yet, there would be the time when those Lightbeings would leave their people and return to the mountain so that they might gather together, so that they might see each other, so that they might nourish each other, so that they might gather about and call upon the presence of the Ones, the Great Ones within.

"Once again, they resided midway upon the mountain. The Great Ones visited them, entering their beings and nourishing them, and the Great Light flowed within and without.

"They rejoiced in the uniting, in the remembering! One being, one people, uniting. One mind. One heart. One being. Rejoicing.

"Then, as before, those Ancient Ones released themselves and gathering their essence together, once again began the journey back to their people. They began to teach the children, speaking little stories so that they might know who they were. There were those who came amongst the children and danced the dance. And the children danced the dance so that they might know who they were.

"There came the day where there were great numbers surrounding the Ancient Ones, those Lighted Beings. A few here, large groups there, two here, great numbers there, and in all, great numbers. They spoke with their people: 'Now I will reveal to you who I am.'

"Then they called upon the presence of the Great Ones who knew everything. They visited upon them, gathering about and entering their beings within and without, and a great light formed.

"Those people who gathered about saw and felt. There were those who, in seeing and feeling, were lighted themselves. They felt themselves change. They felt the knowingness enter their beings. They knew who they were.

"The Ancient Ones then called to their people, saying, 'Come with me. Come with me. Let us gather together.' There were those who ran away, and there were those who came.

"Yes, dear ones, they gathered the people, calling them to come, for there was coming the great Breath of the Earth Mother once again.

"At the time of the Great Gathering, the Earth Mother opened. Those Lightbeings who had been residing within the great Earth Mother, being the Earth Mother, and more, those beings who knew who they were came forward from within to without, and they too did gather. The light of their beings shone as a beacon, calling them all, calling them all, calling them all.

"And there came the day when they did gather together, all. All. Together.

"Yes, dear ones, this is your story."

They heard the words of their dear Ancient One, and even as he spoke, the light about his being grew. Even though there was the morning light about them, his light grew even greater. They basked in it and in his love and knowingness, and they heard their story.

This he shared with them on the morning of the third day of the telling of the truths.

Blessed are you who are hearing this tale.

CHAPTER TWENTY-EIGHT

Those Beings Asleep Did Begin to Awaken

The Midday of the Third Day

After their Ancient One had spoken, at midday they each separately placed their backs against a tree they had used and shared many, many times before. Part of their pattern of living was to sit and be under their own tree at midday.

On this day, even their Ancient One rose and brought himself to the tree which he had used and shared over and over. Thusly, they all did the same.

The People allowed the words and the teachings of their Ancient One to reside within their beings, and there they remained with their trees, feeling the support and sharing and allowing the energies of themselves and of the trees to blend together and be one. They had done this since they could remember, even as children.

As they sat, each one heard the words of their Ancient One speaking with them within their own minds, within their own spirits, within their own heart of hearts. They heard the words: "From the beginning of the end of this day, we will be together in this manner...always. They felt their Ancient One within themselves. They felt his greatness within their greatness, his heart within their heart of hearts, his spirit within their spirit.

As they were sitting, in the center where they had been that morning there appeared a silver form, and once again the being from the planet from afar spoke with them. "My brothers," he said, "long ago, in your time, there were those of us who ventured to the top of the mountain. There we changed. We watched ourselves and each other change in form, in our manner of being, our manner of thinking."

Seeming to answer their questions, he continued, "Yes, even though it was not the place for us, we had traveled there. We were young. We were adventuresome. And we were defiant of the rules.

"In this manner we changed: Our bodies changed. We watched ourselves and each other expand so that our forms no longer presented themselves upon the top of the mountain. And then they were there again. We watched this pulse-beat occur with our own selves. We didn't know these teachings. We didn't know about the midpoint, about the parting of the branches of the trees and the pausing there for merging with the Ancient Ones. We, in our haste to discover, journeyed directly to the top.

"Then for us there was no returning, for we had changed. Our forms no longer carried our spirits in the same manner. We were unlearned. Our heart of hearts had changed. We didn't know of the teachings. We didn't know of the heart unions.

"Since that time, those teachings have become your natural rhythm of daily living. You don't think they are teachings, yet long before you, in the time of your father's father of fathers, there began the teachings of the heart union.

"This day your heart unions flow strongly. Yet we who were changed at the top of the mountain knew not. We felt only cold within our hearts.

"Then there came upon us a swirling that gathered us within it. There we were, not knowing even if we had form, knowing only that our spirits were within a vortex, spinning. We didn't know then of the manner of transformation from one location to another.

"When the spinning ceased, we found we had formed once again, yet we were different. We were nearly as you see us now, and we were standing in a different location. There were those also barely in form who approached us. They were a pulse-beat before our eyes: one moment form, one moment essence. As we looked at our own selves and at each other, we saw that we were the same as those approaching.

"Since that day, in your time there have been three Ancient Ones. During that time, we learned of this new location. Now we called it our beloved Lockspar.

"On this day, there will be forming here with you those of us who so long ago changed and were unable to return to you in our new form because we were unlearned beings. We have learned much in the manner of form and transportation. This day, then, we place ourselves upon the Earth Mother and join with you. This is the first time since we traversed that we reside with you together.

"We are able to do this for two reasons: we have learned our teachings of integration of matter, form and essence; and also, you have changed. The vibrations of your daily living have changed. Thusly, we are able to be together once again, brothers in form.

"We can now say this occurrence is heart-felt joy, for we, too, have learned the teachings of heart joining, even though our form remains quite different from yours. We are amongst you now for this last Gathering in this manner with our Ancient One.

"Thusly, you see, we are the same. Thusly you know, we are the same."

The People heard the words and felt the heart-union. They recognized their brothers and felt the flowing joy. In form and in spirit, they welcomed and received their brothers, those who were the same as they.

Those silver brothers in the center then also sat, pulsating as they were — form and essence, form and essence — yet their spirits remained strong in one. Their light flowed strongly.

When the Ancient One rose and returned to the Gathering place, the flowing between those in the center and his being increased. The light between them grew for they were in union. Form simply moved about; spirit, one and the same.

When he took his place, the others rose also and gathered together. As they viewed those in the center and their Ancient One, their own vibrations increased. They felt themselves pulsating! Light flowed through them.

They felt their forms change a little. It was ever so slightly, and yet they did change. Even as they stood encircling those in the center, they felt the light flowing. What they were seeing they became!

They felt themselves joining. They felt themselves flowing as a river to each other and through each other, within each other. To the center flowing, joining, union. To the Ancient One flowing, union. It was as if they were a river of light.

In this manner they were together, for their brothers had returned, and once again they were one and the same. In this manner they remained and heard their Ancient One speaking with them. It was as if they were his words, and yet they heard his words. It was as if they were his heart of hearts, and yet they felt his love.

He began to speak.

"Oh dear ones, on this day so long ago, a Gathering occurred. Even those who had been observing took form and gathered. Many, many were we, the People, gathered together. We were many forms. From every cavern we came.

"And you, dear ones," he continued, "the father of your father's father, and the mother of your mother's mother and the great Warrior which I was had been beckoned inward. Even though the others gathered together, we went inward. This great Earth Mother opened her being and beckoned us and we did go.

"Thusly we flowed with the breathing in and breathing out of the great Earth Mother. For when the last being stepped from caverns to be upon the Earth Mother, then we placed our first steps within and inward we did go.

"Little did we know of this grand Gathering of beings. Those ones of the light came, bringing those who were still asleep. The People gathered. Upon the dawning of the Moon Mother they gathered, encircling the gathering place. All beings. They glowed, walking about. Every heart bore the Song of Songs of the Gathering.

"They walked the truth of their beings. Into the center of the great wheel they had formed they walked so that they might be spirit without form, and then stepping outward from the center and taking form. This was their great teaching. Into the center of light, disseminating, and with the pulse-beat forming, stepping outward from the center. This they did continually.

"There came then union. There came then, dear ones, memories of a force that had engendered this great teaching of dissemination. In the marriage of dissemination and form came the great teaching that we the People and the great Earth Mother form together.

"Even as the realization of those teachings in that one truth filled their beings — spirit remained, form changed; spirit remained, form changed — those beings asleep awakened. Soon the entire Earth Mother awakened. Glowing, she was.

"Since the beginning of the taking of form, this became the teaching: That the light within took form without. The great Earth Mother felt herself and her People.

"As the pulse-beat of the universe continued, that force of dissemination then presented itself and there were the two forces together: form and dissemination. It was as if there were two Earth Mothers together, each facing the other, one of darkness and one of light.

"In their innocence, the People saw. In their innocence, they opened. Then, as if an arrow in the dark of night, the force of dissemination did strike the People upon the planet called Earth.

"There were but a few who knew of the opening to within, and they gathered those about them and quickly went there into the caverns. Within they went, within and within. There they formed lighted beings. And without, on this great Earth Mother, there was darkness.

"Yet she did spin, and where there had been covering of light, there was covering of darkness.

"Then there came the time when the darkness sought the light. Of your time of counting, dear ones, it had been only thirty days of darkness upon the Earth Mother without. Yet within, it had been three hundred years. And within, there had become a land wherein the People dwelled. There were those who had dwelled under the darkness, and they too found their way within.

"There did come the time then when the darkness found the opening to within and flowed inward. Thus then, while you, your beings, your father of your father's father and this great Warrior were as asleep within the great Earth Mother, there did form a battle of battles: the darkness and the light.

"As the great Earth Mother shook her being, she spun and spun. Through the battle within, great flames formed and covered her being. Hurtling, she spun about in the grand universes. The battle of darkness and light.

"When the darkness had gathered all of itself together, and the light had gathered all of itself together, in a great explosion they separated. The darkness came to without the great Earth Mother and took form, spinning and spinning about. Together they were, united yet separate, as two great balls: the dark upon the light.

"Even as each one was spinning, at last they did separate. The battle, even though it had not been won, was complete.

"You see then, dear ones, this Earth Mother upon which you reside is the new Earth Mother. You didn't know this. You believed that the tales of the tale of the tales of the great Earth Mother were the same. Until this day, we could not speak this truth with you.

"Thusly, that great black moon that you honor and to which you sing the Song of Praise is that form and force of dissemination of the battle of old. And that which you honor, upon which you reside, is that great light form of union.

"In millennia of millennia of millennia, there comes the day when the two — planet of dark and planet of light — join once again. That day will not be for you. For this day you but hear the truth. Even the children of your children's children will not know that day.

"Those who reside on the planet afar of Lockspar have learned these truths. Upon that day, in the millennia of the millennia of the millennia, there will be those who will gather together even the children of your children's children.

"When there will be the union of the planet of dark and the planet of light...then, dear ones, will be birth. Yet even as we be amongst you, we say this is your home. For as those beings did go within, the father of your father's father and this Warrior came forward and resided upon this new Earth Mother — as you. In our gathering know you now: that which was the Land Within did come without! And *that is your world here.* These trees upon which you place your backs journeyed from within to without.

"Yes, dear ones, we gather here."

After he had spoken with them and they heard the story, their Ancient One spoke for them to rest and be. Even as they felt themselves changed a little, they remained amongst themselves and those beings from afar also remained together in the rhythm of their beings.

Thus passed the afternoon of the third day when their Ancient One came amongst them to speak with them of the teachings and of the stories and of their beings.

Blessed are those who hear this tale. Blessed are those with and without form who gather together in the receiving of this tale. For as the Ancient One then speaks with the People, then We, the Ancient One, do speak with you, the People, that you might know your own story, that you might know your own heritage.

CHAPTER TWENTY-NINE

Until There Was but One Remaining

The Last Gathering

Silently, their eyes spoke of the changes amongst them as they looked from one to another and then to their Ancient One. They did so enjoy basking in his radiance, in his very presence, in the flowing of love from his great heart, in the sound of his words caressing them. It was as if he cradled them in his arms and sang softly in their ears.

They had heard that he would no longer be with them in this manner. They had experienced his very being within themselves, had felt his presence and heard his words spoken within them. This they knew, yet with their eyes they spoke of the love they carried for basking in the presence of his physical being.

Thusly, they gathered together that they might be with him. Those from Lockspar encircled the People, forming a silver ring around the Gathering, waiting to hear the words of their Ancient One, perhaps for the very last time in this form.

He returned to the rise standing, towering over them, so grand was he, and outreaching his arms. It was as if he were embracing each one.

There came then one of those from Lockspar, taking form in the center. She gazed upward and upward at his great form, even as she felt the light from his being, felt her heart swelling in his presence, felt the joy within herself in his presence. Even as she recognized the feeling, knowing she was the People, she began to speak. "Oh Ancient One, we have been without your presence on the planet bearing our people, your people, the People. Here, these people hear your truths. Our people on the planet of Lockspar hear not your words, feel not your presence, know not your love. For there on Lockspar we have resided in knowingness and in emptiness. Our people need you. Our people need the feelings you emanate to us. Our people barely remember the resonance of joy. Yet our people reside upon the planet called Lockspar and, as you have said, we are the People.

"Yes, those of us from the start did climb the mountain to the top and experienced the change without the knowing, the quickening without the heart, and the essence of being without the heritage. Thus began our separation from who we are. The returning of the People and the speaking of your words have rekindled in us but a spark. Oh Great One, oh Ancient One, then we beseech you that upon your last word here would next be your first word there. There! Among your people on Lockspar. We beseech you to come!"

The People standing about heard her words, felt her plea, and their hearts opened, feeling deep love for their own brethren of Lockspar.

They looked about at each other and spoke with their eyes, "Perhaps our Ancient One will go there."

He heard them. He heard the People thinking amongst themselves and he heard the words of the one young woman, for she had dared to change herself, to step forward and form before him and to speak the words of the heart.

Even as she was speaking, those of Lockspar responded. Deep within them they felt something again. They hadn't recognized the hope building until it burst from them and did shine a light. And the Ancient One knew.

She didn't return to the outer circle, but stood there, keeping her gaze upon him. Then turning, she faced the others, saying, "Oh People, oh People, release to us your Ancient One!"

Returning her gaze to him, with outstretched arms she sang the Song of Praise of the Ancient One:

"Oh Ancient One,
You have shown us your love.
We praise your love.

Oh Ancient One,
You have shown us the teachings.
We sing praise to you in the giving.

Oh Ancient One,
You have embraced us
And we have felt you about us.
We sing the Song of Praise in the Union.

Oh Ancient One,
You are the People.
We sing the Song of Praise to the People.

Oh Ancient One,
Be you with us ever more.

Oh Ancient One,
You are the top of this great mountain

And the Earth upon which we stand.
Oh Ancient One,
We sing the Song of Who You Are.
Praise do we sing
Upon this Earth, to this Earth Mother,
That she would take form and be as we.
Praises do we sing
even for this Gathering."

Before her last word was finished, he began. "Oh People, gather here." He motioned them to come closer. "The changes are about you and yet you beseech that the changes would not occur! Hear you these words. Those of you who are lost are now found, for you feel within your heart of hearts.

"Know you this: Those who now travel the journey upon this mountain do so with the knowingness that they are the Ancient One. There is but one Ancient One. You are that Ancient One. I am that Ancient One.

"This you cannot yet integrate within your being. You must travel to the mountain. There, upon the journey, you will know who you are. We say: Begin your journey!

"You are beseeching your own selves to be amongst you. Hear you these words? In love we do speak. *You are beseeching your own selves to be with you.*

"Here then, in this the last Gathering of this kind, we begin the journey. Oh great people, you are the People. Your heritage is grand and long and filled with journeys. Your heritage is grand and long and filled with truths. Your heritage is grand and long and there have been many and there have been few, and even in the few have been the many. For each one breathes the breath of the People. Even if there were to be one, there would be many, for you are the People.

"Within and without, you have resided upon the Earth Mother of old. Within and without, you have resided upon this new Earth Mother. You have resided on this Earth Mother of old and raised your hands in the singing of the songs to the Moon of Light, and you have stood upon this new Earth Mother and raised your hands to sing the Song of Love for the Moon of Darkness.

"You have dwindled and you have grown. You have struggled and you have lived. Always there has been amongst you One teaching the teachings, beckoning you to remember who you are, beckoning you to awaken to who you are! Always, there has been One.

"This day, we say unto you: this is the day of awakening. Do not beseech us to stay or to go. Turn to your heart of hearts! Therein resides the One who has been with you always. You think we be that One. You be that One. Yes, dear ones. We bask in each other's presence. We glory in each other's love. We radiate in each other's light.

"Yet we do form ourselves on this day that you might awaken, that you might know in your very being who you are." He pointed. "Thereupon, you see the darkness of your being, glistening, the black moon, the new Earth Mother.

"Thereupon you see! Know you your own darkness. Know you that you have surrendered your darkness so that it might form and glisten about you. Why have you done this? Why has this great Earth Mother changed?

"That there might be the awakening! That you might know who you are! That you might feel who you are. In the depths of your heart of hearts, you are this and more.

"Then we say: In this day, we do then open ourselves and radiate the Light of Lights that you might enter, that you might then be One, that you might then awaken, that you might then place your feet upon the path of the mountain of the mountains. And thereupon, on the journey, you might experience the newness of your being. And thereupon, at the top, you might experience that and much more.

"Then again we say: We open ourselves to you that you might enter!"

Their Ancient One stood and from the very center of his being poured forth a light. It grew and it grew. Golden light. It was as if upon his being, a door had opened and within there was light! Golden light.

The light spread forth, flowing, filling the entire circle, touching them and beyond them, even to the ones of silver surrounding them. And they saw and felt the light of the Ancient One.

Even before they could think of it, one stepped forward, that one young woman from Lockspar, and she walked into the light. They saw. They saw her outline as she entered, and then they saw no more. Just the light.

Again, before they could think, there was one child, laughing, his arms outstretched wide, running into the light and into the depths. And then another and another.

Soon they all were moving, first one and then two, the People as they were and the People of silver, mixed together as if a flowing river, they went. The light beckoned them. They heard the call. And they entered.

Until there was but one remaining, and before the Great Light he stood and said, "Then even unto the last, let us be awakened. Let us know. Let us be. For thereupon I see the darkness, and hereupon I see the light. Let then even unto the last, who be me, enter this light."

He began his walk, and even as he placed his feet upon the Earth Mother, she shuddered just a little. With each step, he came closer and closer, until his outline could not be seen...if there had been but one to see. There wasn't, for he was the last.

Into the light they had stepped and as they entered, they felt themselves stepping within the radiance. They felt themselves, the radiance of their hearts, stepping within the radiance of the Great Light emanating from his being.

They felt themselves change. Where they ended and he began, they didn't know. They felt their own minds thinking. They felt their own spirits being. They felt the depths of their own hearts.

Then they felt the others thinking. All of them, thinking. They felt all of their beings. They felt all of the depths of their hearts. And they felt the One. They felt their minds become One Mind. They felt their minds become One Thought. There was no end of their minds and no beginning of others' or even of their Ancient One. One Mind.

They felt the depths of their hearts come together. They felt the depth of the love of their hearts come together. They felt the depth of the feeling come together, until they were One Heart, One feeling, the depth of One Heart.

They felt the spirits of their beings unite. They felt the spirits of their beings and the spirits of the others and the spirit of the One, the Ancient One, come together, as if in a Gathering, and even more. They were One Spirit, One Breath, One Heart, One Mind, One Being, One Light.

Herein they did reside.

Even before they saw the light racing across the space between the two planets, Earth Mother and Lockspar, those beings on Lockspar did feel — they knew, they heard.

The great Earth Mother breathed and felt the light flowing within her being, and *She healed.* Upon the barren sand, pools of water did spring forth. Upon the great barren rocks, there flowed forth life essence.

Even upon the place that birthed the black of the glistening Moon Mother, there began a flowing. From an opening flowed forth white liquid, flowing as a river. Glistening. Flowing, as if in celebration of the healing, of the union, of the One.

In this manner then, they did be.

Then we open our beings so that within your own selves you might experience the Light of Lights so that you might walk into your own selves.

CHAPTER THIRTY

They Remembered Even More

Against all odds, against all encumbrances, against all attempted hindrances, we have been in the telling of this tale.

There are those who would experience satisfaction with the ceasing of this telling, that the People of this planet called Earth Mother would no longer have the possibility of receiving this tale in a form and manner in which they could take it into their beings as nourishment for spirit, mind and body.

However, there are those who anxiously await the story of their own heritage, the story of their own selves. Their reaching outward, their sincere reaching outward does provide a clear stream on which to flow.

In this manner and with this awareness, then, we continue the telling of this tale.

The Dawning of the Fourth Day

In the history of the breathing in and breathing out of the planet called Earth and of the great universe, there has been the gathering of like together. At times, this has produced even what we would call separation. And yet, with the breathing in and breathing out there have come the greatest separation and the greatest union.

The great dark moon glistened in the sky and the great Earth Mother, filled with light, spun. Those beings awakening upon the morning of the fourth day found themselves as if awakening from a long sleep.

One awakened in the bushes here, another there upon the rock, another there in the field, and another there under the tree. As they began to awaken and move their limbs, they wondered how they came to be so scattered about.

It took but a few moments, and then as each remembered what had been occurring, they filled with the splendor of themselves. They looked about and saw each other, and first one and then another gazed upon the seating place of their Ancient One and they saw that he was not there.

Then they remembered even more. They remembered the union. They remembered the light. They remembered the oneness of them all. They looked again at themselves and at each other and saw their light glowing.

One stood and stepped forward, placing her foot upon the path of the mountain. Then another and another until soon they were all walking upon the path of the mountain. They went upward, upward.

Even though they were together as one being traveling up the mountain, they were also separate. At the midpoint, each one went this way and that way, each as the beckoning called him or her, one to the water trickling down, another to the ferns, another to the boughs of the trees.

Here the story pauses. There is one who wishes to speak with you, dear reader.

CHAPTER THIRTY-ONE

This Is the Truth

They Speak to You, Dear Reader

On this planet called Earth, we speak with you. We are from the farthest planet of this universe of ours together. You do not know of us yet. We know of you. In this universe then, you are the youngest amongst us.

People of this Earth, your planet prepares itself that it might turn. Hear you these words being spoken simultaneously upon this planet. We form here that you may hear the peril of your planet. Through innocence, you have received these words through your prophets, for you knew not what you might do. Some have built shelters; many, many, many have brought their thought patterns to wholeness in the attempt to maintain your planet.

And yet, it is our observation that this Earth will turn upon itself, rolling within its own axis. We here speak with you, for when you gather together for the purpose of creating mind-union, then we come amongst you. Then the choice is yours. Then you may accept our assistance for temporary evacuation during the time this planet turns upon its axis.

We are the same as you. This manner of forming and speaking does not lend us to demonstrate our likeness, yet we are the same. For there have been, in the history of this planet, other times when we have come amongst you. There have been those of you who have accepted our assistance and who also have chosen to remain with us.

In every telling of the story of your heritage, there has been the emptiness that lies in the absence of the full explanation. Those civilizations that appear to have disappeared from your planet are amongst us.

We are the silver beings of which this tale has spoken and we say to you now: This is not a tale. This is the present. This is your hearing. As the tale presents the heritage of your beings on this planet, thus then the history evolves to now. These words are spoken and written even as we speak them in many gatherings of your people of mind-union.

We speak with you frequently as the time approaches. But years remain.

Perhaps you will come to know us better and feel our similarities. Perhaps we will take form more completely amongst you to share unions for the purpose of establishing trust through experience.

For then the time will come and we will come for you at the turning of the Earth, your planet, upon its own axis. Many before you have also come, individuals and groups and civilizations.

This too, then, is your heritage. This, too, then can be your choice. We are the same. We are brothers. Through this medium, then, we speak and in the hearing, then, we begin to know each other directly.

Our planet supports our life form similarly to your home planet called Earth. We have spoken with others upon this planet of Earth. Pages have been written about our words and then the words have been abandoned. In this manner, then, perhaps you will hear these words, for as in this tale of your heritage, we speak with you, for you are the People, and we are the silver beings coming amongst you to speak with you, to say we are the same.

Assistance can come in many forms and has. However, in the years to come, the assistance will be in joining together that you might know us and clearly decide for yourselves. This is not a prophecy of doom. This is meant to be rejoicing in union. For, then, there are those of you who have come in the past and will come in the years forthcoming who will, then, upon the settling of the planet, return.

For this planet is your home. There are those beings of civilizations who wait for the time of return together in union, then, returning to this home. Until that time, our planet and our people offer assistance and temporary evacuation.

Be not alarmed, yet hear these words. Never have you been abandoned. And amongst our people on our planet, never have we been abandoned. Then we reach out to you to begin a union, to begin so that when your choice is at hand, you will know with certainty the correctness of choice of your actions.

For there will be those who will remain, there will be those who will go within and there will be those who will join us.

This tale you have been experiencing is the history of your planet. Even as you hear these words, you are living your history in the present. Even though this manner of communication does not demonstrate our joy, there is upon our planet deep joy and heart-felt rejoicing at the gatherings of beings for the purpose of union. For therein, we join.

This union is the manner in which we reside upon our planet. These unions have shown us and beckoned us as beacons to come.

Then in this time frame, in this gathering, in this tale of your heritage, we breathe our breath upon you. We extend ourselves to you. And again, then, we would come and speak and be that we might know each other, that we might know we are the same.

This is the truth. This is now. This is the present.

CHAPTER THIRTY-TWO

He Placed Both Hands upon the Table

The People then did each place their feet upon the path of the mountain. It had not been something they had actually decided to do. It was that on the fourth day, they found themselves walking upon the path of the mountain, and those from the distant planet continued with them.

The journey up mountain was not one that allowed simply walking and walking. Different places upon the mountain beckoned them: berries here, waterfall there, sitting places.

And yet, even as they did explore this great mountain which had been reserved only for their Ancient Ones, they felt the strength with themselves grow. It was their journey. It was their mountain. All knew within their heart of hearts that they were indeed and in fact, the Ancient One.

Each knew that their Ancient One, their beloved One who had spoken with them, resided within them even as they made their journey up their mountain, up the mountain of the Ancient Ones.

The Door to the Universe

As they traversed, there came a place where one woman sang the song and the branches of the trees parted. There she saw a place of residing and she stepped within. Even as she did, there was a glowing within the place as if it had been awaiting her, awaiting one of the Ancient Ones, and her very footsteps brought it to life.

As it began to glow, she saw about her. There, a table, there in the corner, a great urn, there, vials of oil. As she stepped upon the great mountain, she saw, rolled against the table, a woven covering. She went to it and unrolled it open. Woven there was a story. She opened it all the way and smoothed its edges. She knelt upon it so that she might look closer and she saw, as in a circle, the story. Figures of people were woven into the weaving. A few here and a few there and, as the weaving went around, the numbers of the People grew and grew until, as she followed round and round, she came toward the center. There in the center were golden threads, as if a great golden light were woven into the center. It was bright. It appeared that all of the People had gathered together.

As she placed her fingers upon the golden threads, she felt the strength of the light flow within her. She felt a living truth vibrating, the Story of All Peoples. It was there that she stood, in the very center of the golden threads of light.

Even as she did, she felt herself to be much more than strength. She felt the presence of many about her and there appeared spirits about her. Even as they stood and brushed against her being, touching her ever so lightly, she breathed in their essence as if nectar.

They breathed the breath upon her and soon they became one breath. One being, one spirit, then, gathered the vial of oil and anointed her. Another opened the urn and from it gathered sweet, cool water and placed it to her lips. She drank the sweet nectar of water and felt it flowing throughout her being.

Then another stepped forward and sang the song of her being, honoring her presence, honoring the One, honoring the strength flowing throughout her being. Then that one singing the song did so simply and even in one movement step within her and be with her. She felt the presence within her. It filled her being and was with her.

Then another, swiftly as if with a breath, did also enter. And then another and another, until there was but one spirit being remaining. That one did anoint herself with oils and again anoint the being of the woman wherein all resided. When she had placed the oils on both, then she too did step within.

They then did be together. They breathed the same breath, and the strength that flowed within them all was one strength, one mind, one being, one heart of hearts. Light radiated throughout the entire dwelling place and even spilled forward.

Even as one on the journey up to the top of the mountain saw the light and stepped forward to see what was occurring, the branches of the trees did bend themselves closed, and he turned away and continued on his own journey.

In this manner she stood. In this manner, was presented to her the door to the universe. Even as they were with her, one being together, she felt herself flowing, as if flowing through the skies.

Rejoicing filled her and she saw. She saw in the great universe the planets and the stars. It was as if her being were skipping amongst the stars, and even as she skipped amongst the stars, she saw others the same as she. When they met her gaze and wonderment, they glowed and then continued, as did she.

Caressing the planets with her being, breathing the breath of One upon the stars, in this manner she traversed amongst the universe. Yet she felt a beckoning and returned, filling her being. Those who were within her came without, slowly and gently, flowing from her being, and did stand about her. Then she breathed the breath of herself.

They then moved about her as in a circle, slowly at first, stepping upon the weaving and the stories of the People therein. Gently and gradually, they began to move faster and faster and faster and faster and faster...until, as if there were essence of spirit spinning about her, she did be. Then, as if a breath had entered and left, they were gone. There she was, being.

This then became her new domain. This, then, became her new dwelling place. For on the journey to the top of the mountain, there were dwelling places here and there, beckoning those who would reside within them. And within the dwelling places resided great entryways to the universes. Therein she did reside.

Even as she moved the few articles upon the table, she recognized that this was her dwelling place. She felt as if she had been there before. She recognized the drawings on the table. She touched a tiny ball and it turned to light. She recognized the ball of light. Yes. It was her dwelling place. Here would be the teachings.

It was as if she were the mother of the mother's mother. It was as if she had been in this place for a very long time. Even as she looked about, she laid herself down and rested her being.

The Twelve Tables

The young man traversing had found an entryway to a great cavern, and even though he knew the others were continuing their journeys, it beckoned him. He felt the freedom to explore. He felt it throughout his being, young though he was. Exploring. He entered the cavern. Down it went and in he went.

There, within, he came to a room. It was a great opening. Even as he stepped within, it was so dark that he didn't see that it was lighted a little. His seeing and knowingness became accustomed to the dimness, and as he went around the corner, there was a little light from the outside of the mountain.

In the chamber he saw twelve tables in a circle. At first he simply looked at them. Then he stepped forward a little and with his hand touched one table, feeling its smoothness, cool, hard, smooth. It felt almost like water flowing from the waterfall, yet hard. As he placed both hands upon the table, it began to glow a light green essence that filled the chamber.

He went to another table and place one hand and then another on it. It too felt cool and hard and smooth. It too glowed — golden. Then to another; it glowed red. Then to another, blue. And another and another, until about him were the colors so bright, glowing from each one.

He walked into the center of that circle in which they were placed about. There he found a small, a very small table, and he stepped upon it. He didn't know why he did this, yet it beckoned him and he placed his feet upon it.

Even as he placed his feet upon it, there came a sound. First from one table, deep, vibrating sound. Then another, another sound vibrated from another table. And then another and then another, each a little different. Then all did sound, resonating, vibrating, and he felt the vibrations fill his being.

Then, without another movement from himself, first came one light beaming and sounding, then another beaming and sounding. Soon a pattern of lights and sound formed. Again and again, it played for him. Again and again.

The cavern filled with the lights and the sound. It was as if the sounds and the light traversed within this great planet, within the mountain, deeper and deeper.

Then one table lighted brighter than all the rest. He didn't know why, yet he stepped forward and lay upon it, placing his being there. It was no longer cold. It was warm. It received him well.

He felt the sound of that table vibrate throughout him, deep, resonant. He felt the light. Then it was as if he were moving and yet his being was still there upon the table. He began a journey.

He flowed a journey throughout the innards of the great mountain. About him he felt the great mountain, about him he felt the essence of all the Great Ones. It was as if he knew the entirety of the mountain. It was as if he knew the entirety of all the Ancient Ones upon the mountain.

Then he journeyed within and felt the great Earth Mother pulsating. He journeyed within her and even as he did, he came upon different caverns similar to the one from which he had come. Some were lighted a little. Some were dark. Some were closed.

Further in he went, traveling until he came upon a great cavern. It was dim and yet he felt the presence. It was as if a great cavern were asleep. There he did encircle and view and feel its presence. "A dwelling place, perhaps," he thought. He let it rest and sleep and be.

In this manner he traveled within the great Earth Mother and she opened herself to him. He flowed with her even unto the core. As he approached the Great Light in the center of the core of the Earth Mother, he watched until there was a beckoning to return.

Then, as if in a lightness of breath, he found himself once again on the table, vibrating. He did be and rest his being. He knew that within this cavern would be many teachings and herein for a time he would dwell. Even as he rested his being, he thought, "I know this place well." It was as if he had been there before, yet he knew he hadn't. Yet, he knew it was his dwelling place, and therein he did be.

The Path to Her Home

There was one silver being who traveled almost to the top of the mountain. Even though she was one of them and on the great mountain and feeling within her being the strength of her being and the strength of the Ancient One, she still felt within herself a desire. It was to return to her home, the planet afar. For even though she loved this great Earth Mother, there was something she had to share with those upon her home planet. There was something she had to do with them. This, then, was her one thought as she approached the top of the mountain.

Even before she placed her foot upon the top of the mountain, she paused a little. She felt herself and the mountain. She felt the others. She knew that once she stepped upon the top, then the change would occur. "It has always occurred in this manner," she thought.

Even as she thought that, the top of the mountain beckoned her and she did then, as if with a breath, place her feet there. Therein she did be. Therein she did see a path. It was the path to her home. Even as she did see it, she felt herself moving toward it, as if silver, flowing.

She did see it from afar — her home, glistening, glistening there, awaiting her. "There was much more she would share with them," she thought. "They must know. They must know."

For there were those who had been on her planet of Lockspar over and over, waiting for the planet called Earth to form, to change, to enter the new domain, to vibrate in a manner they would be able to withstand. Yes. She would speak with them. The changes had occurred.

CHAPTER THIRTY-THREE

We Speak with You Again

To the Reader

We speak with you again of ourselves, that you might know more of us, that when that time is here and now and we appear for you, you would with ease and comfort, if it be your choice, receive our assistance.

Our planet, at first glance, would appear to be quite different from yours. First you would see silver, and you might think you were approaching a silver ball within the universe. Then you would see blue. Blue, as your own sky, yet sparkling essence. Then, of course, red, as you know it and call it. It is the glowing natural color of our planet.

Upon entering the atmosphere of our planet, it perhaps would feel a little thick as you move your beings, your limbs, about you. And yet, you would find that breathing is easy and effortless. The density of the atmosphere you would find would support you in a manner different from your planet of home. It is more as substance. Indeed, you perhaps would find joy in stepping upward or outward, as if in the atmosphere. Soon you would perhaps then enjoy ease of movement. That is one difference between our planet and your home planet.

One similarity is that our living growths provide us with nourishment, as do yours. However, that nourishment of one would fill your being for two of your days. Soon, perhaps, you would discover which would be most nourishing to you. These growths, living growths, you would find once you enter the real atmosphere of our planet.

Then from red, you would step forward after a time of acclimation. In the real atmosphere of our planet is what you call gold. In stepping within that atmosphere and breathing within your being, you would perhaps at first find great nourishment. Perhaps you would feel as if you were a child. Your scientists have called this the golden elixir of life. It is, however, the natural atmosphere in which we live.

There are those of us who would approach you and assist you in learning how to live within this added strength and vitality. Our manner of living is much the same and yet much different from your manner of living, for we enjoy total and complete mind-union, heart-union, being-union.

We, as you amongst your planet, did not begin this way. There had been upon our home planet as upon yours in this day, warring factors. Our planet, through the eons, has undergone great changes. Currently, we enjoy union. It is the peace you speak of and much more.

We, of course, recognize there are those of you who would not be quite accustomed to this manner of living. There have been provided dwelling places in which you might reside and there would be those of us who would be your comrades that you might, if you so choose, enjoy learning of mind-union and heart-union.

We would say of ourselves that we are a gentle people. Let not this manner of speaking lead you to believe otherwise. We enjoy relations with each other. Once every thirty of your years, a child is born among us. Our children are our treasures.

We are a strong people. Strong, and there is strength in union. As you move about your day on your planet, we do also, yet a little differently. Within our day, there is great care taken for union with those life forms producing our nourishment. There are those amongst us who are similar to those you call your scientific explorers. We fulfill ourselves in manners similar to you.

We speak this little information that you might be able, if you choose, to think of us in a way we have presented. And yet, we recognize that there is more needed in building trust. This is, then, but a beginning attempt to reach outward to you, to speak with you of our home. We observe you and the status of your planet always, for you are a compassionate people and we are similar.

Then, even as you continue in your regular rhythm of your life, and you perhaps allow your thoughts to drift toward us, then we have begun to communicate together. For speaking is not communicating. Union is communicating on our planet. When you perhaps allow your thoughts to drift to us, then we communicate.

Thusly we present ourselves to you. For there comes the day when we will come to you to temporarily receive you amongst us whilst your planet transforms through change.

Then we would gather in this manner again. Perhaps at one time we would speak the words with each other. Upon that time, our synchronization within this body-physical will be more complete and we will be able to, perhaps, if you so choose, speak words with each other. Yet, in your thoughts of this, perhaps you would know that then begins union.

In this manner, upon your planet of home, we come amongst you."

Blessed be those beings hearing this tale and hearing the words.

CHAPTER THIRTY-FOUR

Some Patterns He Recognized

There was one being amongst them all who traversed to the very top of the mountain without stopping here or there, without feeling the beckoning to go to this cave or to go to that sitting place.

It wasn't as if he had been determined to journey to the top of the mountain, it was that he found himself journeying directly to the top of the mountain, and there he did stand. He seemed to be the same, he felt no different. And the top of the mountain appeared to be simply the top of the mountain! He walked around a little there, feeling the Wind Spirit blowing through his hair. As he stood, he saw something amongst the bushes, and he went there to see. It was a long staff, polished, smooth.

He removed it from the bushes. Indeed, it was taller than he as he tried it out, placing one end beside his foot, grasping it with his hand, standing there. It felt fine. It felt as though it were his. Even as he was thinking these thoughts of how it was and wondering whose it was, he felt a vibration in the staff.

His hand felt it at first. Then slowly he became aware of a humming sound. Soon he felt it surround his entire body. He reached the staff upward, as if to the sky, and there formed beams of light.

One beam of light came from the middle of the staff and beamed outward very far, as if to that distant planet of Lockspar. Then, nearly at the top — nearly — came another beam flowing outward directly to that glistening black moon. Then there formed another beam from that black moon to that distant planet.

This he saw and felt as it happened in a flash. He wondered whether, if he placed the staff back under the bushes, the beams would stop. And yet he stood there holding it upward.

Within the beams formed patterns. Some patterns he recognized. He had seen them before and even drawn them before. Others he had never seen. It was as if they flowed from the staff to the black moon to the distant planet and back again.

Then, as quickly as it had begun, it ceased. He placed the staff back into the bushes. Even as he was moving quickly, he wondered to himself why he was behaving so. He stood again, looking at himself, at the few bushes, and at the flat rock upon which he stood.

"This is the place," he thought, "where the Ancient Ones spoke with each other. This is the place," he thought, "where the Ancient One received the visions. This is the place," he thought, "where the others had transformed before their time. Here."

He felt his being changing and as he viewed himself, he saw that first he was not and then he was, as if in a pulse-beat. He held up his hand and saw that first there it was and then it wasn't, and then it was before him again! He felt himself changing.

Then the next thing he knew, he was forming, forming anew, somewhere else. What was this place? "Where am I?" As he took form and looked about, he saw silver. "This must be," he thought, "this must be the home of our brethren, Lockspar."

He didn't see the bushes — or any bushes. He didn't see the rock upon which he had been standing or any other rocks. He didn't feel the Wind Spirit blowing through his hair or any other movement. He simply saw silver.

Silver and a type of structure, glistening. It was not that it was unpleasant. It was that it was very different. Just as he took form, there seemed to be a tiny beam of light coming from one structure. A being, much like the friends he had met upon his home planet called Earth, a silver being, approached him.

He felt the words within him, although he didn't hear a single sound. He felt the words within, "Welcome. Welcome." He felt himself moving toward that being. "Come," the being said. He followed it into the structure and felt it close behind him.

It was bright in this place. Quite bright. Then he saw them; on the walls, all about him, large, large symbols. He recognized them as the same ones that traversed within the beams of light.

"Come," the being said, "come." He still didn't hear a sound aloud, and yet he followed. Through another entryway they went together, into blue, shadows of blue, essence of blue, blue light. He felt it around him. Before he could examine it or think about anything, the being said, "Come."

Through another opening they went, weaving their way here and there through a corridor. The being said, "Here," and pushed open another entryway, motioning for him to enter. This he did.

There it was. "Red," he thought. "The sky is red, red glowing." It reminded him of his home planet, yet it was different. Others appeared before him. Once again, even though he didn't hear the words he felt them. "We were hoping you would come here."

He thought, "This appeared to be the one choice — and not even a choice! It seems as though there I was, and now here I am!"

One being thought to him, "You could have chosen the black moon."

Yet he knew within himself that he was here and this was where he should be.

Then the one who had welcomed him said with his mind, "Soon there will be a meeting of the Council. We welcome you."

He thought, and he felt, and he knew, "Yes. Yes, I will come."

They prepared for him a place in which he might reside, with the glowing of red, and they assisted him to journey there, holding him by the arms. There he rested until the calling of the gathering.

At the meeting, all were present. This time, he heard them speaking aloud. Even though he was within a container of red, red light, and they were without, he could see them and feel them and hear them clearly.

One said to him, "This red light is temporary. It is used to acclimate you so that you might be in our atmosphere comfortably."

They met together and said, "There is a great difference, one great difference between your planet, Mother Earth, and our planet, Lockspar. Here, it has seemed to you that you have resided here with us but for this part of your day, and yet when you return, there will have passed the number of three hundred years, if you were to even return in this day."

He heard the words. He felt the words. And he felt the knowingness. He knew it was the truth.

"We are your people. We are the People also," said another.

This he knew to be the truth.

"Within a winking of an eye, it will be time."

He turned and looked to see the one who was speaking.

"For there comes the time when we gather together and present ourselves to those beings, the People, upon your planet called Earth, the Great Earth Mother.

"For once again, she will shake herself free. We present ourselves to her people, our brethren, that they might be lifted and carried to here. Temporarily. To reside here, temporarily, whilst the great Earth Mother does turn once again.

"Even upon the morrow, in your awareness, if we were to begin on the morrow, even then it would be five hundred and twenty-three years since you last placed your feet upon the great Earth Mother.

"You will barely recognize her. You will barely recognize the People. Many, many they will be. Many. For the great Earth Mother is in the purpose, is destined to carry upon her many. Then we would come."

He heard the words. He felt the words. The expanded being of himself, the expansiveness of his being, did know it to be the truth.

"During this time of preparation," said another of the Council, "there will be those messengers who visit upon the planet called Earth Mother to speak with the People there, to tell them. There are those who will believe. There are those who will not believe.

"Those of us who will speak with your people have left before you arrived here, and they will arrive closer than a decade to the occurrence, so that they might speak with the People upon the Earth Mother."

Then one did say to him, "Then we say to you, what has brought you here?

Why are you here? Can we help you?"

He did be. Then he felt the beginning of himself to speak and it grew and grew until he was quite ready. When he did begin to speak with them, he didn't know what he would say, yet he knew whatever it would be would be the truth. Then he did speak with them:

"Upon the great Earth Mother, I have resided for many turnings of my life. It has been the journey to the top of the mountain that has revealed this to me. I have resided upon the great Earth Mother in the forests, wherein the trees were my home. I have resided on the great Earth Mother in the sands, digging for roots. I have resided within the great Earth Mother in the caverns. And I have resided deep within the Earth Mother, in the Land Within. I have resided in the waters of the great Earth Mother.

"I know her well. I understand your changed concepts of time. And yet, upon traveling to the top of the mountain, I learned that all time, all residings, occurred even as I saw them, and which occurred first was not plain to me. Which occurred presently was also not plain to me.

"One week perhaps appears to be of great value with relation to that planet of my home, called the Earth Mother, yet I am here. I have come here to free your thinking. I have come here that you might directly, through your own selves, experience joy.

"And yet you say, 'How can this be?' I too say, 'How can this be?' For it appeared that merely a moment ago I was standing atop the Great Mountain...and in the next breath, I am here.

"Yes, we will return to my home planet. Yes, we will return together. Perhaps, perhaps many years will have transpired. Yet I know the truth of truths: that we can locate the year from which I traveled and return there."

They heard his words. They felt them. There were two who wept. And he did be.

They Speak with You Again, Dear Reader

We have come amongst you in every possible form, in every method, to speak with you. For the time of gathering and the time of remaining and the time of going within will be yet a number of years.

Yet there can be those who journey with us to our planet to see, to feel, to experience, and to return to you to express their findings. In this manner would be one way of building the trust between our two peoples and with our planet.

This journey can occur within your time existence, for we have learned to accommodate ourselves to the vibration of your planet and your manner of being. There are those who are being approached for this purpose. There are yet others who see our traveling apparatus as their own personal initial contact between us and those of our planet.

Perhaps you would consider within yourselves if you be one to make this journey. There will be other meetings as this before we would ask you of your decisions.

Then we will remove ourselves from your presence until the next communication. We have greatly improved the synchronization in communicating.

CHAPTER THIRTY-FIVE

It Is Our Heritage to Continue

That one being from the planet of Earth who resided on that new silver planet called Lockspar rested and thought about himself and his surroundings.

He was functioning properly, he determined. His awareness was able to encompass his surroundings. Yet he was unable to join with the minds of those with whom he had just communicated. That apparently was one factor of difference between his relations with his home people and these new people calling themselves his brothers. "However," he thought, "perhaps this is temporary."

He observed himself and felt a peace throughout his being and, sighing a sigh, he settled to rest. "Not to sleep," he thought, "simply to rest." Yet thoughts of the words came to him of the rescue spoken, rescue of the People upon his home planet, and of the difference of time — so long — occurring even now as he thought.

His being craved for the natural vibration of his Earth Mother, for this waiting place in which he resided, even though it was comfortable, left him a little empty. Perhaps it was his being accustomed to his great Earth Mother.

"It was the vibrations," he concluded. "It was the vibrations themselves that were different here. Of course they would be," he thought, "it is another planet! Another way of being!" Then he truly did rest, even from his thinking.

He stayed with the people of Lockspar, learning their ways of being, accustoming himself to the new vibrations, until there came the day when he could walk amongst them freely and clearly. The vibrations of the planet of Lockspar and his vibrations had become totally and completely compatible and communicable. He freely walked about.

Even in his walking around the dwellings in which they lived, he still longed for something. One of them came to him and they spoke together.

She said, "Come, I will show you that which you long for."

As if in a blinking of an eye, there appeared before him a grassy knoll. He smelled the air about him. He smelled the grass in the air. He looked around. Yes, there were the trees. Yes, and the running waters. Yes, even the birds! His being filled with overflowing joy. It was as if he were viewing his home.

She spoke with him, walking as they did amongst the grasses and blossoms, saying, "We have created this for the People of the planet of Earth Mother. We will create more so that those coming here might assimilate themselves in a more familiar environment, that the living upon this planet, our home planet of Lockspar, will be most comfortable for them.

"Here you can fill your heart," she continued. "Here there is the vibration of your Earth Mother and our Lockspar, together. Here, we can be one mind. We have felt your wanting to join," she said to him. "And yet within our own vibrations, there still would be great changes for you. Still, perhaps by the time we then traverse again to Earth Mother, you will be able to experience mind-union and heart-union within our vibration. However, here we can."

Even as she spoke with him, he felt the union beginning and the flowing between the two. Even her silver glistening being melted with his, and they experienced together one, one mind, one heart, one being. Yes, this was what he had thirsted for.

For since the union upon the Earth Mother and the traveling here, the emptiness had grown. Yes, this was the feeling, the nourishing – one. His being rejoiced and the one which they formed rejoiced.

Those beings of Lockspar recognized a union occurring and those beings of the planet called Earth felt a union occurring. It cause them to look at each other and to embrace each other...and to be.

The Meeting of the Council

Then there came the time when, during the meeting of the Council, he, the being of Earth, was beckoned. As he walked amongst them, he felt familiarity, comradeship. He knew them well. He had been there for ten of his years.

He thought to himself, "If even the counting here were the same...," laughing a little to himself. Even though he had been there for some time, when he looked at himself, he felt no change.

He came amongst them at the Council and they spoke with him of his great Earth Mother and of the changes thereupon and the increased number of the People.

They asked him if he would speak with his people and prepare them within their beings so that they might prepare themselves. "Yes," he said. He would speak with them.

They all stood in the circle in which they had been sitting. Even as they stood, there emanated from them great light. It was as if the light from them and around them formed a woven egg of light, as a dome, vibrating.

They motioned him to step forward and speak.

He felt their love and he felt their caring. He felt their deep concern for those of the Earth Mother. And he felt deep within his heart of hearts his wonderful Earth beings.

He stepped forward and this he said to those upon the Earth Mother, those of One with whom he had stood that day, those with whom he had traversed upon the mountain, those residing on the Earth Mother, and those of the Ones who had walked upon the great top of the mountain:

"Oh People of the Earth, I am told there are many of you. I am told we have grown in number. If this be true, then perhaps still there are those who remember this one, for I am of the Earth Mother. Then I speak with all peoples of my great home, the Earth Mother.

"And I speak with those who remember who I am and who we are. I speak with those who remember the union with the Ancient One. I speak with those who remember and feel this day One – One Mind, One Heart, One Spirit, One Being.

"And I speak with those who did, with me, place our feet upon the great mountain and journey upward. And I speak with all peoples upon this great Earth Mother.

"And I speak with those beings whose home has been Lockspar and who now do reside upon the great Earth Mother.

"Hear these words: There will be the day when our great Earth Mother, as in the heritage of old, will spin herself free. Then the breathing in and the breathing out occurs again in the breath of this great universe.

"In the heritage and history of this great Earth, during the times of breathing in and breathing out of the great Earth Mother, those who reside within shall come forward and those who reside without shall enter within.

"Yet, this day I do say to you: Here, upon this distant planet, I be. For to the top of the mountain I did travel and from there to here. And here I reside. For us all, I remain here.

"Then hear these words: Upon the beginning on the great Earth Mother of spinning and breathing in and breathing out, then these beings of Lockspar will present themselves to you that you might join them. Glistening silver are they. You would but gather together, those of you who so wish, who so choose.

"Those of you who choose the Union of One, hear these words: For the breathing in and breathing out of our great planet continues evermore, and yet there is the Gathering as there has been of the Union of One. Then, upon that time, our brothers, our friends, our comrades of this planet on which I reside, will gather you together and bring you here.

"I have been here and am here. We can live here. A place has been provided for us. Then, when the great Earth Mother settles again, we shall return. In this manner, dear ones, we are able to continue our consciousness of One. In this manner, we can continue to remember who we are. In this manner, we can continue to be the Ancient Ones. In this manner, then too we can continue to gather those about that they might awaken and join in the One.

"This day I speak with you, even though I stand amongst these beings of this distant planet called Lockspar. I feel you hearing these words. I feel you remembering our union. I feel you remembering the mountain. I feel you remembering the Ancient Ones amongst us. Yes, beloved Earth brethren.

"Again and again will I speak with you, and then even those of this planet of Lockspar will speak with you. I feel comradeship with these beings upon this planet. Feel within yourselves these feelings from me to you. Determine for yourselves. And then begin to carry within your being the knowingness of the upcoming times, without fear, without great concern. And with great union, with the knowing, with the remembering, with the communion, with the remembrance of who we are. Yes!

"For it is our heritage to continue! It is our heritage to be One — One Being, One Mind, One Heart, One Spirit. This then, I have said to you."

In gatherings upon this great planet called Earth, the words did resound. And there were those who heard and felt the union. There were those who heard and wondered. There were those who heard and remained asleep, for the numbers had grown.

Those upon the great mountain heard and knew and felt and did be the One. The light and the vibration of that union filled the vibration of the Earth Mother, and those living there did lift their manner of being.

Blessed are those who hear the words of this telling and feel the One.
Blessed are those who awaken.
For you all, we speak this great tale,
for you all.

CHAPTER THIRTY-SIX

Missing Persons?

It would appear by this time that all those who hear this tale would have recognized that they are in deed and in fact the People. It would appear perhaps that stirring within your very heart of hearts, you perhaps even wish it were your story. And, in deed and in fact, it is!

This then is the true history and heritage of this planet called Earth and the People residing upon Earth: You. You all — yes — *are* the People.

There do come those to you from the distant planet afar to speak with you. Yes, you hear, and wonder at the reality of these words. And this we say: This is the truth. The words are the truth. Yes, presented here are the words for you to hear.

Here are those "missing persons" who wish to speak with you:

Howard Trevor Taylor

"Dear beloved people of Earth, my fellow people, my name is Howard Trevor Taylor. I disappeared from this Earth on December 2, 1875.

"Known as an eccentric during my time, rather than a scientist, I managed to keep most of you away. Not that I did not care for those of you, but to keep your questioning eyes and minds from my work.

"I had been communicating with nonphysical beings for a number of years. Even though I believed my journal and entries would be formed into documents and then printed and published for the world to see and read, my main thrust of communication was to discover other living beings upon other planets.

"The work I produced initially was quite similar to the writings that have appeared upon this planet recently from nonphysical beings. However, there was one transmission that came unlike the rest. This transmission appeared to be from other living beings. I daren't tell even those few who knew of my work of that latest experience, for at times, I believe those few did come amongst me to assure themselves of my sanity.

"Yet in the secrecy of my own laboratory, I did then communicate. I did then communicate for a number of weeks. And then, difficult though it may be to believe, I received instructions to travel, to be at a certain location at a certain time on a certain date, that date I have given you as my disappearance date. For there I did be.

" 'Twas at night. I was alone. I thought to bring with me different scientific theses, different books of literature, different spiritual writings. I did not. I brought nothing but myself. And there I stood.

"Just a tiny thread of doubt existed in me. And the rest, expectation. And I was fulfilled. For there, above me in the sky, what appeared to be a star grew larger and larger until it came to me, moving quickly and oddly. And then, without my even seeing its approach, it was above me.

"It did not touch this Earth. Light, light came from around the edges. And it appeared as if the light were a support. And under and in the center, a large column of light. And there, it was there I had been instructed to go.

"With the smallest amount of hesitance, I stepped under, there in the light. Then, I could effectively say, I disappeared from this planet.

"Amongst them I have been on that distant planet. You of Earth have not seen this planet, have not discovered this planet. There I have resided for in years the number nearly five. Here, of course, on this planet has evolved approximately a century. This is the difference in time.

"Why have I remained here? I became accustomed to the planet. I became accustomed to the People. And I met other people from Earth there who had also become accustomed. Why were they there? Why did I remain?

"The People of this distant planet did prove to me, through the history of the existence of Earth, upcoming changes. From there on that distant planet, we could calculate the approximate number of years. Those others and myself are now presenting ourselves in this manner.

"The purpose of our presenting ourselves is to alert you of upcoming changes. And to alert you to even more — to alert you to the wonderful possibility of temporary evacuation. I know that when I lived upon this great Earth, not one of you could I convince of anything you would not be convinced of! Not one! And I suppose that's why I am here trying to convince you, even though perhaps it is futile, of the truth of the words being spoken within this tale. It's called a tale. It could very well be a historical novel, a history book of the Earth. It would present greater truths than ever printed before.

"I am here to tell you, to speak with you, to assure you of the genuine offer of assistance. I am here to speak with you and to tell you of the genuine safety offered. I am here to dare you to adventure! To dare to adventure! Rather than perish! Rather than perish! Dare to adventure!

"There are others from Earth who reside on this distant planet. They too speak, some directly to their loved ones, others to groups of people. In many different manners, all of us residing upon the distant planet will continue to speak with you and attempt to provide for you the words that will allow you to choose adventure! Rather than perish.

"It is the deepest pleasure, even in this manner, to reside for these few moments upon my beloved Earth. The time draws near. But years remain. And upon the distant planet, but breaths. Yes. We await you with open arms, beloved friends. Dare to adventure. Dare to live. Dare to go beyond the regular structures of living. I know you can do it. I know you can. You needn't be a crazy eccentric as I, so they said, in order to adventure beyond that which you are.

"I look forward to greeting you at the gates, with open arms. You only would make the step. Take the step. Reach out and grasp helping hands.

"Until then, I bid this great Earth and my wonderful people adieu."

Kathryn Henrietta Freestone

"My name is Kathryn Henrietta Freestone. I disappeared from this planet in the year 1743. Truly, I was seeking refuge from those who believed my demise would be their benefit. I journeyed in the dark of night through the dense forest and to the bog. There, truly, I did not know what I would do. In the bog no one followed me.

"My husband, believe you that he was an alchemist. Yes. And even upon his death, I entered his rooms and read his papers, his thoughts on paper. He spoke of other planets and other beings, living beings. I don't really know if he even had proof, or if it was his thought. Yet, part of his thoughts became my thoughts.

"And yet, the fleeing. In the fleeing I had forgotten everything, everything. I didn't know what I would do. And yet, there I was in the bog. And a deep humming came from the bog. It was actually quite loud. It frightened me a little. And then the lights flashing, different colors, much brighter than lanterns.

"And I couldn't run to where I had run from, and so I crept around a little closer. And there it was. Silver. Silver, bright silver, glowing. Nothing I'd seen before. And there was an opening. There was an opening. And there was light coming from the opening.

"And truly I have no idea what possessed me ever to walk there and into that opening. I simply did it. Thinking of George all along. My husband. Thinking of him all along, I did step into the entryway.

"Well, there, much to my utter surprise, were other beings. Strange. Glowing. Yet the feeling I had with them was great comfort. And then it felt as though we were moving, and of course we were. And before I knew it, from there, from my home to their home, I went.

"Since then I have resided on that distant planet. I have changed much. I have learned much. I have become much. And I come here to speak with you in this manner. To speak with you and tell you: Their offer is real, it is genuine. There are quite a few of us from Earth there, on their planet, waiting until the Earth does change so that we can return. It utterly amazes me, what I have experienced.

"And I have seen through their observations what has occurred here on Earth. Through this experience, I still am a young woman. I genuinely speak with you to encourage you to come. To come. I look forward to seeing you soon.

"A place has been made for you, for us all, on that distant planet. It is not difficult to live there. It's simply becoming accustomed to something a little different. And then we can return here, if we want. I do so want to be on Earth again. So, do come."

Jack Kelliher

"My name is Jack, Jack Kelliher. I disappeared from the Earth January 2, 1954.

"I left...well, I was flying my plane, drifting about, and I see this disc just...might as well have been a strange story right out of the books!

"I wasn't dissatisfied with my life. I was ready for something else. Never knew this'd be it, though. I heard them speaking in my mind. I even shook my head to be sure it wasn't something wrong with me. Took off my headphones. And they were talking with me, asking me if I wanted to join them. And I said, "Why not? Oh Jack, why not?"

"It's as simple as that. They moved, flew that thing right on top of my plane. Before I knew it, there was a hole right there. And before I knew it, up I went! Off I went.

"Well, they were different, all right. Fairly nice folks. Got to know each other right quick. And away we went! Oh, they spoke with me just as I'm speaking with you. Told me there were others like me on their home planet. And I says, "Oh yeah? What they doing there?" They says, "Want to meet them?" And I says, "Yeah." So, away we went.

"There are quite a few of us. Quite a few of us. And we've all really worked together to make a place for you all, anyone who wants to come. I don't even pretend to understand all of their figurings out, but I can tell you this: there's going to be some big changes. This I know to be true. And there's a place for any who want to come. Any of you. It's right nice. It's a right nice place.

"And then, they say, when it's all over we can come back to Earth. Begin anew. I don't know what old Jack Kelliher will do. But I'm up for it. And what am I talking to you like this for? To tell you it's a right nice place made ready for you. We did it together. We did it together.

"It's a little different; it's a lot like home. I can say this, Jack Kelliher never knew, when he thought he was ready for something different, that it'd be this different! And I'm just telling you folks, come on along. Come on along. Then we can come back here and begin again.

"And don't bring anything with ya! Everything ya need is here! Everything. Just come on along. See you there! Come on."

And the Council Was Pleased

And the Council was pleased with the young one who had spoken to his people. They surrounded him and embraced him. And one said to him, "Come. Another comes from your great Earth. Come. Let's greet him." Together they went to greet the one.

Those of the Council looked about at each other. Joy. Their faces shone with joy at another who had come. And one said, "May there be many more."

Blessed are they who hear the words. Blessed are they who receive the words. Blessed are they who carry the words to others that they might hear, that they might carry the words to others, that all might hear and might know. And all might choose to be the Ancient One.

CHAPTER THIRTY-SEVEN

It Is a Time of Rejoicing

Howard Reeves Schmidt

"My name is Howard Reeves Schmidt. I disappeared from Earth and my regular living on December 2, nineteen hundred and forty-two (1942).

"In my life, I have borne many different names, for I was known to be a genius. I was known to be a creator, an inventor. At first, in my young life, I learned how to play the game with those impressed with my talents. I played with them as I did with my inventions.

"Then, as my inventions grew to be more useful, I became their prisoner. At first chance, I ran, ran away with but my manuscripts. The rest I burned. I stayed hidden for three years in a tiny village near Stockholm. Then I was discovered again. And in the night, when everyone else slept, I was taken. In my life, I have run away and been captured forty-three times.

"One of my inventions carried the purpose of communicating beyond this plane. Beyond! There came the day when there was communication. I hid this fact from everyone. I made no notes. No recordings. And even the drawings of this invention were labeled falsely.

"I climbed. This body had been broken many times and yet I climbed. I climbed! For the one salvation in my life. And there, atop one of the smaller mountains, I did meet these people with whom you have been speaking. And that day, December 2, I did go with them.

"When I left this planet, our planet of Earth, I was sixty-seven years of age. Since I have lived on this distant planet, my vitality has returned. My broken spirit has been mended. There, there, oh fellow people, there exists no harm, a dream I have carried for this planet, our planet. Perhaps one day it will be here.

"I have thrived and am thriving on this planet afar. And I come here in this manner which I have learned, to speak with you. There are many from Earth. We live together there. When the time comes, if you choose to go, you will not regret it. There were those of my friends who stayed when I left. Perhaps they have not regretted it either. I can only speak of the going. And I say again, if

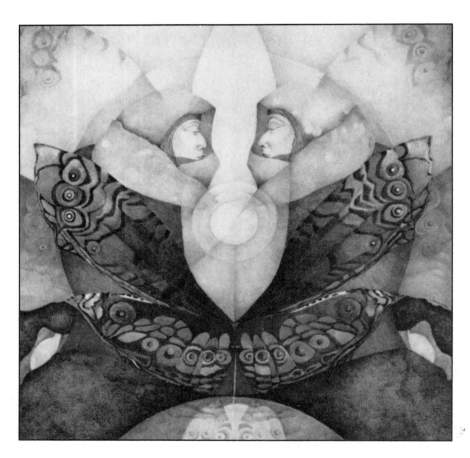

To the Flame

"There will be the Gathering where you will be presented with the opportunity of mind-union, heart-union, spirit-union with those from the distant planet."

you choose to go, you will not regret it. For when the time is done, then we can return and begin again.

"I have changed there. All of us from this planet who have lived there have changed. We are learning how to live without harm and with union. We changed people will return and begin anew. And I call you to come and join us. There is nothing like this Earth."

Being from Lockspar

"I am from the planet you call the distant planet. There are those upon your planet who prepare themselves for upcoming changes upon your planet. As we have been speaking, there are those who would go – that is, to come with us. There are those who will stay. And there are those who will go within.

"For those who choose to stay, we offer these words: For a time you will be able to live upon your home planet. Then you will be unable. There will be no place to run to. And those you hope to help will not reach you. We do not say these words to harm you, but to alert you to the immensity of change that will occur upon your planet.

"Yet those who remain will be, for that time, of great assistance, since they have chosen to remain in order to help those who do not understand what is occurring. Yet, know this to be true: There you would then reside until the next breathing out of your home planet.

"These words we speak with you to assist you in your decision-making. These are but our observations. However, for many, many, many of your Earth-centuries, we have observed and we, with certainty, present these words to be truths.

"In your hearts, in your minds, in your spirits of being, there can be rejoicing and joy for the upcoming changes. There has been one of you from Earth amongst us who has taught us joy. For hearing the words is different from experiencing what the words are saying. And throughout our people, we include with our unions great joy.

"We realize that this information can be startling, can be ignored and perhaps can be considered. We simply present ourselves for your assistance, if you choose."

A Time of Rejoicing

And so, dear ones, you hear your own story. You hear your own heritage. And you hear those beings speaking. Yet we say unto you: Even those beings from the distant planet called Lockspar began here upon this planet called Earth Mother. You are all the People. You are all the People. And you who hear these words? Yes. Yes! You are those Ancient Ones.

Many journeys have you made. Many journeys do you step upon, even now. Yet we would speak with you of your beloved home, Earth. For within this great Earth Mother resides the birthing of this grand universe. And within your very self resides that universe. This is not a mystery. It is your heritage! It is your truth of truths.

Blessings be upon you who hear these words. Blessings be upon you who hear these words and carry them to others. You are what you are and much more. Have you not had an inkling of this even in your daydreaming? But of course.

Deep love there is for you, for there are those who gather about you to assist you in even your thinking of these words, the story of the People.

There will be the Gathering where you will be presented with the opportunity of mind-union, heart-union, spirit-union with those from the distant planet. The purpose would be to assist you, and through the experience, perhaps then you would speak with others.

For it is a time of rejoicing!

CHAPTER THIRTY-EIGHT

The Decisions

The People on the planet called Earth Mother heard. The People on the great Earth Mother felt. The People on the great Earth Mother knew. For she did rumble beneath them and her waters rose and fell with great magnitude. The People knew.

There were those who had traversed the great mountain and then placed their feet again upon the land from which they had come, and they carried the truths and the knowingness with them. Then they bore children and their children bore children. Soon there were the children's children's children upon the great Earth Mother. Even within them was the knowingness carried of who they were.

There were some who traveled about this great Earth and then from them came children's children's children, and they too walked upon the Earth Mother. They danced upon the Earth Mother. Yes, they sang praises for the Earth Mother. They were many.

They felt and knew and saw the Earth Mother changing. Her pulse-beat was different. They felt it quickening beneath their feet. They felt her and they spoke with her. Those who had traveled within traveled within and felt her. Yes! This great Earth Mother was forming anew. They felt it and they knew it.

There were those who gathered together, speaking amongst themselves, one saying, "Now. Now is the time that we must decide what we will do, each one of us in our heart of hearts. For we have been told some will remain, and some will go within. We have heard the speakings of that wonderful Land Within. Our heritage speaks to us. Our songs speak to us. Our stories speak to us. Never have we been empty of our stories.

He continued, "This day I say to you, then, I am thinking and preparing and deciding whether I will remain, whether I will go within, or whether I will traverse to that distant one afar. Even though we have not seen the distant one, I do know within my heart of hearts the truth of our heritage. The truth of the weavings of old. The truth of our songs of praise. And the truth of our visions which we have shared amongst ourselves. Our dear friend has traveled upon this Earth Mother and has returned with stories and visions of others, and even words from afar. Upon hearing his tales and upon hearing those words and stories, within myself I knew them to be true. "Then I say to you, this be the day. Then I will decide, choosing within my heart of hearts. And I say to you, my friends, my people, my family, perhaps it is for you to decide also. For feel you the Earth forming anew beneath you? Feel you? "There are those who have journeyed to the mountain and therein resided — and returned. They have seen the Earth from afar. They have seen the Earth from within. Yes. Forming anew, she is, our great Mother Earth."

They heard what he said. They knew what he said was the truth, and yet there were some who thought it would never come to this. Some who thought it would never come to deciding. They looked about themselves at the Earth and felt her, even as he spoke, and looked above at the great sky and about at the trees. Yes. The great Earth Mother was changing herself.

For hadn't the trees...hadn't the trees been so different this season? Carrying their blossoms far into the cold, bearing fruit in the dead of cold? And leaves falling in the beginning of warmth? They had seen. They had spoken amongst themselves even as they covered themselves and gathered the fruit. Thinking, never before had it been this way.

Yes, these changes had prompted ones to travel to the mountain once again, to place their feet on the journey. A sitting place beckoned them and therein they entered and heard the teachings and asked the questions. "What is occurring? Oh great Mother, what is occurring?" They saw and they knew. She was changing herself.

"Yes," they thought, "this could be the day that they would decide what they would do. This could be the day."

Then another spoke with them. "I have been traveling and have heard one from the distant planet afar. I have seen the silver form of that being and have heard the words. That silver form, that being, said there are but years and even less now. That being spoke of the planet afar and of the place made ready for us, a place where we might live and nourish ourselves until this great Earth Mother forms herself anew. Even though we decide in our heart of hearts, I, for one, have decided." He looked about at them. "I have decided. Even though I don't ask you to share your decisions with me, I say to you, I, for one, will go to the planet afar, there to reside and wait upon this great Earth Mother, to wait for her to form herself anew. And then I shall return. That is what I have decided!

"This I have decided because I saw that silver being take form. I heard her voice and I knew her words to be true. For in our stories and in our histories and heritages, and in the song of songs that we sing, we sing of our friends, our brothers, the silver beings who came amongst us. You see?

"I have awakened even more. I no longer sing the songs. I be them. I know them. They are truth. This then is my decision."

At the Mountain

It appeared that upon the great Earth Mother, gatherings formed here and there, small and large gatherings, the People speaking amongst themselves of the decisions to be made, for they felt and they knew.

In the Gathering closest to the great mountain, the People gathered.

They viewed their great mountain. Many had traveled there and in the traveling had decided what they would do. As they gathered, one stood and spoke with his family, his friends, his people:

"My friends, I speak with you so that those who decide as I might gather about so that we might make ourselves ready, as did those of our father's father long before us made themselves ready. For was it not those, even before this great mountain, who, at a moment's notice, left their belongings and gathered themselves and followed their visions and entered this Earth Mother? Are they not then, our family? And do they not be our father, our mother, our Ancient Ones? Are not we, the People of this great Earth Mother, born of them?

"Then this I do decide. Upon the day of beckoning, then I leave everything and gather my family, my Old Ones, as the story has been told to us, and my children, and carrying but ourselves, we shall go within.

"For in our heritage we hear the words of this great Earth Mother who breathes in this universe. We have heard of her breathing in and breathing out, and hereupon the People have lived through the breathing in and through the breathing out. Then, upon this next breath, I do rise and I do enter.

"There, deep within the Earth Mother, I have seen this Land Within in my traveling through the great mountain. There, the ways will be open unto me and those who be with me, and we will travel within upon the breath of the great Earth Mother and reside within.

"There are those who are deciding to travel to the distance afar. My brothers, I know your decision to be correct as I know my decision is correct. It is my truth. Yes, there are those of you who will remain here.

"Here then, I present myself, for the assistance in preparation of those who will remain here. For when I ride upon the breath of the Earth Mother but myself I will carry. Then I say, where are the preparations?

"For there are those within the wildernesses who will come forward to us, beseeching assistance, for perhaps they have not heard the words. Perhaps they have not heard the words! Perhaps they don't know of these choices. We know there are those in the wildernesses.

"Those of us who remain give our assistance until that moment when we depart."

Within the Caverns

Within the caverns, they prepared. Foods. Water. Clothing. Coverings. Oils. They prepared. Even in the preparing they knew that those who remained would perish in the folding and unfolding of the great Earth Mother as she formed herself anew.

Upon Lockspar

Those upon that distant planet of Lockspar knew of the decisions, for the time of preparation for those beings on Lockspar was complete, and they began traveling to the great Earth Mother. Even as they began, they gathered about. Those silver beings and those many, many from the Earth Mother gathered about and viewed her.

They began the journey. Those of the Earth Mother, in order to assist those coming so that they might see each other and recognize each other, gathered in each vehicle and began.

In the score of three hundred they began. Their observations and their calculations led them to the moment so that in their journey, when they arrived upon the Earth, it would be at the time of change and there would be those waiting for them.

Union

And then, dear ones, we say to you: In your heart of hearts, perhaps there is a decision forming for you? Not that you would scurry about, but that you would know within your heart of hearts your decision.

For when this great Earth Mother begins to shake herself free and mold herself anew, then will be the moment.

Then, dear ones, blessed are they who have heard the words in the telling of this tale.

We say unto you, now there come the beings of silver in spirit form so that you might experience mind-union, heart-union, one, so that you might feel within you and then you perhaps could decide...either.

Then even as you are reading these words, if it be your choice, simply be and make room for that silver being. Pause and feel the union of heart and mind, for through experience you can decide. Now, pause for union. Just be and allow it to occur, for the spirit be with you now.

CHAPTER THIRTY-NINE

The Visions

Your Ancient One Speaks with You

On this day, this be a composite of those who gather about you in guidance, in care, in love, in union. We take form together many, many, many times for you, the People. We have also taken physical form and come amongst you. This day, we come amongst you in this manner. In this way then we are your Ancient One.

We speak this day of visions, of movement, of union. All forming of words this day simultaneously forms matter, for the vibration of truth resides and takes form through the spoken word. Of such power is the spoken word.

In the times to come, this truth will be your tool amongst all others. For the vibrations upon this home planet called Earth increase momentarily and increase and increase. Those who vibrate within the awareness of expansion and union gather together the essence of the truth and speak the word.

Demonstrations of this truth occur in daily living. When you, the People, awaken and use this truth in consciousness, greater proofs cannot be than these. Words take form.

The First Vision

See you this Earth as from afar.
See you its colors,
See you its spinning.
See you its glow,
See you the flames,
See you the rolling ball of fire.
This, then, be the first vision.

The Second Vision

See you white essence flowing from within this Earth to without,
Covering.
See you the white Earth.
This, then, be the second vision.

The Third Vision

See you the great of breaths blown
upon the Great Earth.
See you the People embracing
your Mother Earth.
See you the People residing
upon the great Earth Mother...
People.
Then know this to be the truth.
These, then, be the visions.

Then these Ancient Ones before you speak of movement,
for hear you these words:
Gather yourselves together,
Know you who you are.
Gather yourselves together,
See yourselves together,
For the gathering begins.

From every corner of every location
In every dimension
Come the People.
See you those amongst you
Who bear the light of their being.
See you this light within yourselves.

Hear the call.
Know you the sound.
Know you the feeling
Within your heart of hearts.
Wherein there be a gathering,
Therein you be.
Wherein you be within a gathering,
See who you are.
Know yourselves.

For there would be the day that those within the Gathering would be scattered about, and each one would be asked to come. And there would be those who, for fear of separation, would say no and return to the Gathering but find themselves the only one.

Then hear these words, for when you hear the beckoning, then come. The others will also come. Follow your heart of hearts. Each one will have the opportunity to come. Fear not, for those whom you loved also are asked. Soon, then, we come amongst you. And soon then, there be the lifting away.

For unto your own self, you are the Ancient One, as we. For you are the People. This tale spoken here is your heritage, your story, your truth. Even before three years will come the time. Bear not this within your heart as disaster. Bear within your heart union. Bear within your heart union.

We accompany you always, for you and we are One. The calling of you will continue for two years. Gathering together. There will be those of you who will remain to assist those to gather together, and yet then the call will come to you and you will know. For not one being would come upon another's call. Yet each of their own.

This we say unto you, the People. For this day, you know who you are. Then this day, let there be union of mind, union of heart, union of being. That we might be One.

The Time

Then they did approach in their silver vehicles, some larger than others. The People felt their presence approaching, and upon this great Earth Mother, they gathered together as they had planned, each calling to each other, "Come along, come along."

There were those who watched and remained. Yet, they assisted them all to gather together. The silver bird approached, spinning about, and the light flowed forth. In the light stood ones, beckoning them, "Come. Come along. Now is the time. Come."

First one and then another, bringing only themselves and nothing else, began to move toward the light and toward those beckoning them to come. First a few and then a few more. Soon, a steady stream, coming, coming, coming....

There were those to greet them and to assist them to enter. "Enter! Enter into the glistening silver."

In every part of the Earth Mother the Gatherings began and the enterings into the silver birds, into the silver balls, into the silver domes, into the spinning silver. Some very large, and some taking but a few. For wherever they were gathered together, then they did come, even unto the ones atop the mountain.

The People of the Earth Mother who would go to the distant planet called Lockspar did then, did then, even on their last step on the Earth Mother, did feel the vibration under their feet. They felt the movement and they knew. The time was at hand. They knew it to be the truth.

Even in the trees, in the mountains, in the waters, the shaking occurred. Even those who had been hesitating, at last decided. "Yes, then we will go. Those of us together, we will go."

Soon the silver lifted from this great Earth Mother and there were those remaining who saw the sights of them carrying the People away. They too knew it to be true. There were those who, even as the last glimpse of those silver birds left from their sight, gathered themselves together, thinking, "Yes. It is time.

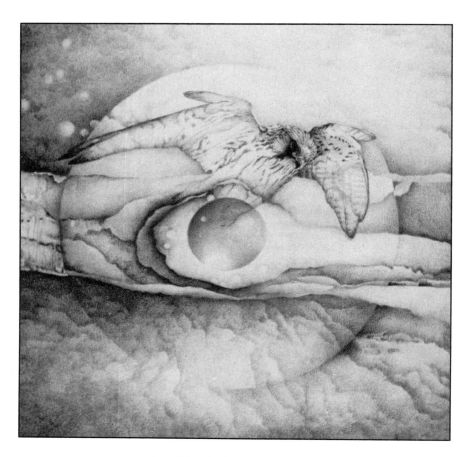

Herald of the New World

"In the rumblings and in the spinnings, the vibrations upon the Earth increased and she began her journey toward newness, toward cleansing, toward birth, toward new domain."

We will begin the journey to go within. Come along. Come along."

And those who had been wondering knew they would go within. Only themselves did they carry. And they gathered about them their Old Ones and their children and looked about at their great Earth Mother.

Even as they looked here and there where they had gathered together, the Earth opened, parting herself, and they praised the Earth Mother for receiving them.

When they looked within, they saw the caverns and the walkways and they stepped within. With the truth of knowingness within their hearts, they began the journey to the Land Within.

For three days there were those who gathered together and entered the entryways, even unto the last of those who would journey within.

On the fourth day then, the openings did close.

There were those who remained upon the Earth Mother and, gathering themselves together, did sing the Songs of Praise.

They sang the Song of Praise for those Brethren, those Peoples, who had departed in the skies.

They sang the Song of Praise for those Peoples who had entered the great Earth Mother within her caverns.

They sang the Song of Praise for themselves,

for those few who remained.

And they sang the Song of Praise

of the great Earth Mother.

The Songs

Oh, People who fly from our sight,
Oh, People who leave through the silver birds within the sky,
Let ye be carried to the distant Planet afar and thereupon reside.

Oh People
Within our hearts,
Within our minds,
We are the same.

Oh, People, our brothers,
Who travel within the caverns
Of this Earth Mother,
To that land in our heritage told,
With you we go.

Oh, People,
Within our hearts,
Within our minds,
We are One.

Oh, People,
Here we do gather,
And sing our Songs of Self,
For we remain.

For the being and the spirit of the People
Remain within and without this Great Earth Mother.
Oh, great Earth Mother,
We sing the Song of Praise
Of your being.

For you have borne us
Upon you and within you.
You are our nourishment.
You are our life force,
For you and we are the same.

Praise be to you,
Oh, great Earth Mother,
For we feel you within us,
Moving.

Oh, great Earth Mother,
Then we do place ourselves upon you,
That we might be One.

The great Earth Mother felt the words and heard the words and knew the words and was the words. She felt ones, those dear ones, depart. She felt ones, those dear ones, enter deep within. She felt ones, those dear ones, remain. And she did spin.

In the rumblings and in the spinnings, the vibrations upon the Earth increased and she began her journey toward newness, toward cleansing, toward birth, toward a new domain. And therein she would settle herself. Yet, even though she knew this, she was just beginning to spin, to shake herself free...to be simply the great Earth Mother.

Again, if it would be your choosing, there would be one come amongst you for union so that you might experience, so that you might feel, for the purpose of growing trust.

Blessings upon those who hear this tale. Blessings upon those who hear this tale and speak the words. Blessings upon those who gather together that they might be one. Blessings upon those who open that they might be in union. Blessings upon those who remain asleep, for even unto the time of awakening, we do bear you in our arms.

Then, as before, simply be, if it is your choice, in union with those beings from Lockspar who say:

"If you choose, then we unite in joy that you might experience the wonder called joy upon our beloved planet afar. Many upon your planet called Earth are experiencing unions such as this. Then we would begin, if you so choose."

CHAPTER FORTY

So Be It

In the telling of histories throughout the ages, in the speakings of stories from one generation to another, in the telling of even family heritages and histories, each speaker speaks that part of the history and heritage which resonates within himself or herself.

And each listener hears that part which resonates within himself or herself. In this manner, then, the truths are shared from one to another and then to another...and then to another.

Now it is not that that which is shared is false or true. It is the essence that is shared that is the truth. The essence. For when each being speaks of the stories and the histories and the legacies with the life force flowing through them, then they are just that — and then each being is carrying the essence to those who are hearing.

Yet, in the histories and heritages of the stories of the planet called Earth and the People residing therein and thereupon, there have been bits and pieces of these histories and stories given to us here and there. Sometimes there have been presented entire stories from beginning to end, and other times there has been a little piece of the entire picture.

And we, as thirsty beings, have taken that drop of water upon our tongues and found that our thirst was not quenched. We wanted more! Yes. Much more!

This is the nature of truth, forging a path for itself amongst us. And when we feel it enter our being, when we hear the truth and feel its resonancy, we open wide that we might hear more and receive more, that we might know.

Thus it has been in the sharing of the history of this Earth and the heritage of the People. In this telling of the tale, the Story of the People, has resided truth. This is the heritage, the truth, the breathings of the great Earth. This is the heritage of the great People within and upon this great Earth Mother.

Yes, we have said that this story occurs even as we speak the words. It is true! Yes, there have been words beseeching the People and also beseeching you who hear these words to awaken! And to know who you are.

To dare to reside at the top of the mountain.

To dare to traverse amongst the stars and planets.

To dare to traverse to that distant planet.

To dare to traverse within the Earth, to reside in the Land Within.

Perhaps you would answer the beseechings. Perhaps there is one part of the history or one part of the heritage that resonates within you so strongly that you must share it with one other. Then, know beyond a shadow of a doubt that that is what it is like to feel the truth resonating within you. To feel it!

Perhaps it excited you because it flows through you. Because it is you. Because it is your heritage! Yes, dear ones, yes.

Then, when this story is completed in the speaking on this day, then begins once again the telling of the tale, the Story of the People. For the Story of the People has no beginning and no end. It simply is evermore. As the histories and heritages roll upon each other, thus then exists the Story, for it is truly the breathing in and breathing out of this grand universe.

And those residing within the great Earth Mother? Yes, they did find the Land Within. Yes, they do reside there, even as we speak these words. Yes, upon their entrance to the Land Within, the Land itself awakened and sparkled once again.

And yes, there are those beings of Earth who reside upon the distant planet called Lockspar. They have begun anew there, perhaps waiting. Perhaps waiting to return to this great Earth Mother perhaps there to remain...and then onward to yet another and another. For their journey is one, the adventurers, onward and onward.

And yes, the great Earth Mother resides, ever she is. When the breathing in and the breathing out require that she shake herself free and be, then, and perhaps only then, will you know, dear ones, if the visions given to you were your truths.

Then we say to those deep within, in the Land deep Within:

"Oh dear ones, prepare yourselves. For once again there comes the breathing in and the breathing out of this great Earth Mother. And it is not the remaining or the going that is the heritage, 'tis truly the union of one. 'Tis truly the union. For therein lies the story. Therein lies the heritage. Therein lies your truth. The union, one. One mind, one heart, one spirit, one being. One."

This then would be the completion of the words of the telling of the tale, the Story of the People, and yet, we say to you, dear ones, that there are many, many, many who gather together here amongst us even as we speak these words, so that they might be in the presence of the last words of the telling of this tale first spoken aloud in its completion in this form.

For in the end of the speaking of the word, in the very next breath and second, is the taking of form. You see?

In this manner then, those gather about so that there might be then rejoicing. Rejoicing from within. Rejoicing from without. Rejoicing from afar. Rejoicing here. And that there might be union. For amongst all purposes in the telling of this tale resides the one purpose: Union. Union. Together. One.

Then we would say it has been our honor to gather together in the presenting of these words and these teachings and this history and this great heritage.

Then, there would be one who would speak with you and with the others who have gathered here. Know you that many gatherings occur even at this second, for we are together. One would speak with you and then there would be union, as in the great heritage when ones felt the Ancient One within them ever more, then thus shall we be...evermore...in union together. As it is always. Always. Never apart. Always together.

He spoke. His beckoning had resounded throughout the universe. They came. Once again His great form stood with arms outstretched, his deep voice resonating: "For it was that we called upon the essence of life to enter those beings, that there would be the coming forth in form. This then has been done." His last word echoed through all chambers everywhere. His last word continued for what seemed like forever. It rumbled within Him even before the sound came forth. All heard. "Aaaamen."

"Then let there be upon this day, upon this moment,
those who gather together.
One Mind...
One Heart...
One Spirit...
One.
Awaken, all Earth beings!
Prepare to receive the words of your heritage.
Awaken, oh Earth Beings,
And receive your heritage,
That you might be who you are!
And that all might be One.
So Be It."

About the Author

Author, lecturer, hypnotist and deep-level channeler, Eileen Rota has been working in the field of spiritual explorations for over 20 years and channels as many different energies.

Her experiences as a psychic child were explored in the magazine, *Venture Inward*, published by the Association of Research and Enlightenment. Her channeling story is told at length in Henry Bolduc's book, *Journey Within: Past Life Regression and Channeling*. Eileen's work is also explored in two books by Henry Reed, *Edgar Cayce on Channeling Your Higher Self* and *Developing Your Psychic Ability*.

Eileen's first book, *Welcome Home — A Time for Uniting* (also on cassette tape) contains the delightful stories, meditations and teachings of the channeled energy known as Pretty Flower. In his forward, Sir George Trevelyan states, "...a fine example of channeling at its best...of profound significance for the spiritual awakening of our time."

Eileen was the four-year director of the Welcome Home Center for Spiritual Unfoldment, located in the Blue Ridge Mountains. Virginia provided a home base as she traveled the East Coast for about seven years, conducting and channeling transformational workshops, classes, retreats, individual intensives and sessions. Eileen is a dynamic speaker and her channeled sessions are alive, unique and fulfilling. For more information or scheduling: P.O. Box 3112, W. Sedona, AZ 86340; (602) 282-2321.

About the Illustrator

Janneke Verster was born in the Netherlands. She worked for many years in textile art, ceramics and sculpture. In 1984 she began to use colored pencil to create paintings which she called soul portraits —works which emerged from a deep intuitive connections with the individual commissioning the painting. Since coming to America, Janneke has been deeply inspired by the landscapes of the Southwest and by the visions described in the book, *The Story of the People*. Her colored pencil paintings, along with the oil paintings of her husband, James Yax, are featured in an audio/visual presentation entitled *Innerscapes — the Journey Within*. For further information about her work, contact Janneke at P.O. Box 1294, Sedona, AZ 86339; (602) 634-6167.

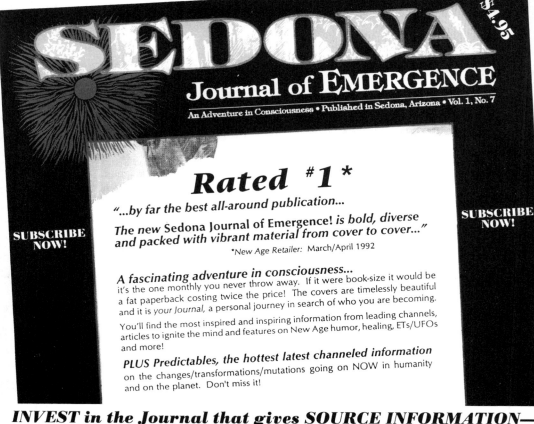

BOOK MARKET

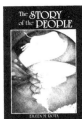

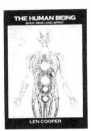
BOOKS BY VYWAMUS / JANET McCLURE

BOOKS BY LYNN BUESS

TO ORDER SEE FORM AT BOTTOM OF PRECEDING PAGE.

BOOK MARKET

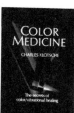